YORK NOTES

THE PROLOGUE TO THE CANTERBURY TALES

GEOFFREY CHAUCER

NOTES BY MICHAEL AND MARY ALEXANDER

 Longman

 York Press

The right of Michael and Mary Alexander to be identified as Authors of
this Work has been asserted by them in accordance with the
Copyright, Designs and Patents Act 1988

YORK PRESS
322 Old Brompton Road, London SW5 9JH

PEARSON EDUCATION LIMITED
Edinburgh Gate, Harlow,
Essex CM20 2JE, United Kingdom
Associated companies, branches and representatives throughout the world

First published 1998
This new and fully revised edition first published 2005
Second impression 2005

10 9 8 7 6 5 4 3 2

ISBN 1-405-80708-3

Typeset by Pantek Arts Ltd, Maidstone, Kent
Produced by Pearson Education Asia Limited, Hong Kong

CONTENTS

PART ONE

INTRODUCTION

HOW TO STUDY A NARRATIVE IN VERSE

Studying a verse narrative in medieval English on your own requires self-discipline and a carefully thought-out plan of work.

CONTEXT

In 1700, the poet John Dryden called Chaucer, the first English poet to have been read in every generation since his death, 'the father of English poetry'.

- You will need to read this short work more than once. Read it through first for pleasure, and then read it more slowly and thoroughly.

- Read the poem aloud in an imitation (however bad) of the historically appropriate pronunciation. (If possible, try to listen to a recording.) By practising thus, and sounding the final -e when the metre suggests it, metre and rhythm can be found (see **Extended commentaries**). This helps with understanding the meaning and the tone of what is said.

- Look up the meanings of all the words you do not know. Some words which survive into modern English have changed their senses. Some may use more than one meaning. Some require notes to explain them.

- On a second or a third more careful reading, make detailed notes on the characters, and on subjects which recur in the narrative. Further readings will help you memorise details and will develop new thoughts.

- In the early stages of studying a text of this kind, it is better to read part or whole of the poem aloud than to read critics. First try to make parts of the poem familiar to your eye, ear and memory. Then you are in a position to discuss the text with others or to read criticism critically.

- Divide the narrative into its principal parts and see whether the narrator plays the same role in each of these parts.

- Is the narrator's point of view one which we are supposed to accept at all times?

- Do some ideas and values come up again and again? If so, do these need to be explained by reference to historical beliefs or different social and cultural situations?

CONTEXT

The Canterbury Tales was not a printed book for eighty years after its composition. It existed in manuscript, or rather in a number of manuscripts.

- In exams or essays, support your argument with brief quotations or details of the text. Try to find your own quotations: it makes the essay so much more interesting for the examiner!

- Always express your own ideas in your own words.

These York Notes offers an introduction to the text and cannot substitute for close reading, followed by a critical study of secondary sources.

READING THE PROLOGUE

The Prologue, also known as the General Prologue, forms the introduction to *The Canterbury Tales*, which has become the most popular work of the most popular English writer of the Middle Ages, Geoffrey Chaucer. In it Chaucer tells us how one April he was staying a night at the Tabard Inn in Southwark, meaning to begin his pilgrimage to Canterbury next morning, when a company of pilgrims came in, and he joined them. He then describes each of the pilgrims in turn, in a set of portraits which remains the most famous extended piece of character-drawing in English. It is done in an entertaining and informal way. The pilgrims all agree to a proposal by the Innkeeper or Host that they should take part in a game: each is to tell a tale on their ride towards the shrine of St Thomas of Canterbury, an archbishop who in 1170 had been murdered at the altar of his own cathedral by agents of the king. This general introduction to *The Tales* as a whole makes sense on its own. In only 858 lines, the Prologue offers a brilliantly coloured, animated and detailed picture of English social life in action.

> **CONTEXT**
>
> Pilgrimage: a journey to a holy place, from Latin *peregrinus*, wanderer. Christian pilgrims travelled to Jerusalem from the fourth century.

Geoffrey Chaucer, who died in 1400, is the first famous English poet. There had been English poems for 700 years before him, the Old English eighth-century epic poem *Beowulf* for example. But Chaucer is the only medieval English poet known to most later poets. He perfected a new kind of verse in English, the five-beat, ten-syllable line used by Shakespeare – and Milton, Pope, Wordsworth, Tennyson, Eliot and many more – and still in use. He is also the only English poet to have been read continuously since the Middle Ages, surprising and delighting new readers in each generation.

SOCIAL HISTORY

Some lasting impressions of the Middle Ages come from the General Prologue – pilgrims on horseback, the *parfit gentil* Knight, the hunting Monk, the lady Prioress, the thin Clerk of Oxford, the Pardoner selling his fake relics, the Wife of Bath looking for her sixth husband, the Miller looking for a fight, the ideal Parson, the good Ploughman. The pilgrimage begins in a tavern in Southwark, and is to end in Canterbury Cathedral. Pubs and churches are

CONTEXT

The poet John Dryden wrote in 1700, in the Preface to his *Fables*, 'Here is God's plenty! We have our forefathers and great-grand-dames all before us, as they were in Chaucer's days.'

institutions which England inherits from the Middle Ages. The company of pilgrims is linked by good fellowship and the excitement of a spring outing. The pilgrimage to the shrine of St Thomas à Becket at Canterbury was the most popular in England. The pilgrims go to seek the holy martyr who has helped them when they have been sick, but many of them are also on holiday. The Prologue is a comprehensive picture and full of life. It is the first page in English social history, rich in detail and colour.

The liveliness of the Prologue owes much to Chaucer's eye for personal detail, his sense of humour and his style. It was a good idea to give a miscellany of stories the form of a story-telling competition, and a better one to make the tellers a group of pilgrims riding along a road. It was a stroke of genius to have twenty-nine pilgrims be so kind as to include him, their creator, in their company. At the Tabard he speaks to each of them and becomes one of their company. By speaking to him, they speak to us.

The General Prologue is a lovely text, fresh and unacademic. But it is also packed with social detail which needs some study if it is to be fully appreciated. And Chaucer's English, though it is largely intelligible, also needs a little study to bring out its meaning, implication and flavour. This is a short but richly rewarding text.

PART TWO

THE TEXT

NOTE ON THE TEXT

The text of the General Prologue is found in all complete manuscripts of *The Canterbury Tales*. There are more than eighty manuscripts of the *Tales*, the text of which breaks up into ten Fragments. The major manuscripts begin with the Prologue, part of the *First Fragment*. No manuscript seems to date from Chaucer's lifetime, but two manuscripts with a full run of tales, known as the Ellesmere Manuscript and the Hengwrt Manuscript, are dated within ten years of Chaucer's death in 1400. These are regarded as close to Chaucer's texts and are the basis of modern editions, though editors also take readings from later fifteenth-century manuscripts. Medieval texts differ from manuscript to manuscript. The Ellesmere is handsomely illustrated with miniature portraits of the pilgrims and of Chaucer. These portraits have become famous, and often feature in discussions of the *Prologue*. *The Canterbury Tales* were first printed by William Caxton in 1477, and have been reprinted in every century since then.

CHECK THE BOOK

The Ellesmere portraits are reproduced in *The Canterbury Tales: Illustrated Prologue*, ed. Michael Alexander (1996).

There is currently no single edition of the Prologue on its own. The edition used as a basis for the present book is *The Canterbury Tales: the First Fragment*, edited by Michael Alexander, Penguin, 1996. This has the text of the General Prologue in a helpful format with, on facing pages, a very full glossary. Besides the General Prologue, it contains the other parts of the First Fragment of Chaucer's *Tales*: the Knight's Tale, the Miller's Tale, the Reeve's Tale, and their Prologues, a total of 4,420 lines in all. It also has an introduction, and full notes.

The standard single-volume edition of Chaucer's complete works is *The Riverside Chaucer*, third edition, edited by Larry D. Benson, Oxford University Press, Oxford, 1988. The text is in double columns, with glosses at the foot of the page and an excellent full glossary at the back. It has good introductions and very full and scholarly notes. A handy edition of *The Canterbury Tales* is edited by A.C. Cawley, Dent, London, 1958, revised Malcolm Andrew,

1996, with marginal glosses but with few notes; and notes are especially useful for the General Prologue. There are many editions of *The Canterbury Tales*, complete and selected, and of individual tales and groups of tales.

Many students use translations. But translations tend to substitute for the original, and it is dangerous to rely on them in preparing for examinations. Good examination answers quote the original text, and the translation will often give a wrong sense. Translations of verse into verse inevitably misrepresent the sense as well as the music of their originals. This is particularly the case when translating from an earlier stage to a later stage of the same language, as the translator cannot avoid using modern English words descending from the words in the original, though the modern word will often have changed sense (see the discussion of the portrait of the Prioress – **Extended commentaries, text 2**). Chaucer is full of nuances and little jokes which are also lost in translation. Finally, a translation is not necessary, for Chaucer's English in the General Prologue, a short text, is not difficult and can be enjoyed after very little study by any speaker of English – or of French, German, Flemish, Dutch or other European languages.

The authors of these Notes advise students to *avoid* translations of the Prologue.

Suggestions for further reading are found towards the end of these Notes.

SYNOPSIS

The Prologue has three parts: a short introduction, the series of portraits of the pilgrims, and their consent to the Host's proposal of a tale-telling game.

Chaucer tells how, at the Tabard Inn in Southwark on the night before his pilgrimage to the shrine of Thomas à Becket in Canterbury, he fell in with a company of twenty-nine pilgrims. These he describes in some detail, in the famous series of portraits. He follows the conventional division of medieval society into 'estates' and introduces them in the usual order: the

CHECK THE BOOK

The Canterbury Tales: Illustrated Prologue, ed. Michael Alexander (1996) also features later images of the pilgrims, including Thomas Stothard's 'The Pilgrimage to Canterbury'

military estate, the clerical estate, and the estate of the workers (Latin *pugnatores, oratores, laboratores*: fighters, prayers and workers). This last estate has the most pilgrims, introduced roughly in order of social precedence. Chaucer ends with a group of rogues, putting himself last.

At the suggestion of the Host of the Tabard, they agree to tell two tales on the way to Canterbury and two on the way back to London; the best tale is to earn its teller a free supper at the Tabard on their return. The pilgrims accept the Host as judge of the tale-telling game. When they set out next morning, the pilgrims draw lots to decide who shall tell the first tale, and the Knight wins. The Prologue ends with the Knight about to start his tale.

A brief account of the rest of the *First Fragment* and a briefer sketch of the rest of the *Tales* may be of use. The Knight's noble tale of Palamon and Arcite is admired, particularly by the nobler pilgrims, and the Host invites the Monk, as senior churchman, to tell the next tale. However, the Miller, who is already drunk, insists instead on telling a bawdy story about the cuckolding of a carpenter. The Reeve, who is also a carpenter, angrily answers with a bawdier story about a miller. The Cook then begins on a still bawdier tale of an apprentice and a prostitute, but the *First Fragment* of the Tales ends when the Cook has scarcely begun.

> **CONTEXT**
>
> 'Canterbury' was originally 'Cant-wara byrig', the borough or town of the men of Kent. It was here that English Christianity began, in 597.

This pattern of solemnity followed by comic and even ribald chaos is echoed in more than one of the remaining nine Fragments of the *Tales*, in which twenty-two more pilgrims tell their varied stories, including Chaucer himself (who tells two) and the Parson, whose tale, a long treatise on Christian penitence, ends the collection. *The Canterbury Tales* thus comes to an end before Canterbury is reached, and before the tale-telling competition has completed the first of its four stages.

The Canterbury Tales, then, is incomplete, perhaps because of the poet's death, although other works of his are unfinished. But the shape of the work is clear. As in other medieval collections of popular stories, such as the Arabian *Thousand and One Nights* or the *Decameron* by Boccaccio, an older Italian writer whom

CONTEXT

The first Canterbury Cathedral, a Roman basilica consecrated by St Augustine, was the seat of the Archbishop of England's southern province, the north being adminstered from York. The Gothic Cathedral dates from 1067.

Chaucer may have met, the primary story forms a convenient framework to a miscellany of many different kinds of tales: romances, fairy stories, bawdy tales, sermons, saints' lives, beast-fables, allegories. However, this frame-story, as it is sometimes called, has a life of its own. Some of the tales are dramatic expressions of the characters of their tellers, and the events of the pilgrimage are sometimes of greater interest and significance than the tales. Human life was often thought of as a pilgrimage, an image which gives Chaucer's work a symbolic meaning of a kind very common in the Middle Ages.

The General Prologue (so called to differentiate it from prologues to individual tales) is the general narrative introduction to *The Canterbury Tales* as a whole. It sets the scene in spring, the season of pilgrimages, and introduces Chaucer as a pilgrim at the Tabard Inn. Then follows the series of portraits of individual pilgrims, from the Knight down to the Pardoner. Finally we meet the Host and hear his proposal for the tale-telling competition. The next morning the pilgrimage sets out.

DETAILED SUMMARIES

INTRODUCTION (LINES 1–42)

LINES 1–18 FORMAL OPENING

In the spring, when flowers grow and birds sing, people long to go on pilgrimage, and the English particularly love to go to Canterbury, the shrine of St Thomas.

Medieval romances often open with an evocation of spring, but Chaucer's description is scientific, astronomical and classical, and his first long sentence is elaborate and formal (see **Extended commentaries, text 1**).

GLOSSARY

1   **shoures** showers

     soote sweet, gentle

2   **droghte** dryness

3   **veyne** vein, vessel of sap

     swich licour liquid such

4   **Of which vertu** that by its power

     engendred generated

     flour flower

5   **Zephirus** god of the west wind

     eek also

6   **Inspired** breathed life into

     holt wood

     heeth field

7   **croppes** the growth of leaf (*not* crops of wheat or barley)

     yonge young (Aries is the first sign in the solar year)

8   **Ram** the sign of Aries

     half cours the second half of its course

9   **foweles** birds

10   **ye** (pronounced ee-ye) eye

11   **So ... corages** so much does Nature prick them in their hearts

12   **longen folk to goon** people long to go

13   **palmeres** pilgrims (those going to Jerusalem wore a palm)

     straunge strondes foreign shores

14   **ferne ... londes** remote shrines known in various lands

15   **shires ende** corner of (each) county

16   **wende** make their way

17   **blisful martir** blessed martyr. Thomas Becket (also called Thomas à Becket, afterwards St Thomas of Canterbury) died as a witness to the Christian faith in 1170, put to death in Canterbury Cathedral by knights of Henry II of England.

     seke seek

18   **holpen** helped (a saint can intercede with God for sick people who pray to him)

     seeke sick (identical rhyme)

CONTEXT

Becket had been Lord Chancellor, the chief officer of state, but when he became Archbishop of Canterbury, the head of the Church in England, he defended the Catholic Church against the king. Canterbury, two days' ride from London into Kent, immediately became one of the chief places of pilgrimage in Europe.

? QUESTION
How does Chaucer get to know the pilgrims, and what is their reaction to him?

LINES 19–42 AT THE TABARD

Chaucer joins a company of pilgrims staying at the same inn as himself.

GLOSSARY

19	**Bifil** it happened, befell
20	**Southwerk** the parish on the south bank of the Thames opposite the City of London, to which it was linked by London Bridge
20	**Tabard** Tabard Inn, a hostelry, bearing the name of a short armorial coat
	as I lay while I was staying
22	**corage** spirit
25	**sondry** various sorts
	aventure chance
28	**wyde** spacious
29	**esed** accommodated
	atte beste in the best way
30	**shortly** in short
	wente to reste was setting
31	**hem everichon** every one of them
32	**anon** soon
33	**made forward** (we) made agreement
	erly for to ryse to rise early
34	**ther ... devyse** in the way I shall recount to you
36	**Er that** before
37	**Me thynketh it** it seems to me
38	**condicioun** state, circumstances
40	**which** of what occupation
	degree social rank

THE PORTRAITS OF THE PILGRIMS (LINES 43–746)

LINES 43–78 THE KNIGHT

Heading the military estate is the Knight, a mounted, professional soldier, and a devout example of Christian chivalry and of the military virtues. He has fought honourably both for his earthly lord and for the Lord of all Christians, campaigning along the whole frontier between Christendom and *hethenesse*, from Southern Spain right round the whole east end of the Mediterranean and also east from Germany, along the Baltic coast into Russia. Despite his prowess and his undefeated record, he was humble and courteous – 'a true, complete and noble knight' (line 72). He offers thanks for his safe return from campaigning by going on pilgrimage.

The Knight's virtues and his roll-call of campaigns recall the ideals of the twelfth-century Crusades: expeditions to regain the Holy Land from the Muslims, led by knights from northwest Europe. The Knight has fought only against Muslims, heathens and schismatics, not (as his real-life contemporaries had done) against fellow Catholics in France and Spain. He is a superlative example of a type virtually extinct in Chaucer's day. That may be part of Chaucer's point. Each pilgrim is a superlative example of his type. If the Knight's achievements are checked against dates and places, they seem too good to be true. But Chaucer was drawing an ideal.

> **CONTEXT**
>
> Jerusalem was taken from Byzantine Christians by Arabs in 1071, retaken by the First Crusade in 1099, lost in 1187, retaken in 1229 and lost in 1291. The Crusades ended in defeat in 1396.

GLOSSARY

43	worthy of proven valour and virtue
45	riden out go on campaign
46	Trouthe integrity, fidelity to obligation
	fredom noble generosity
	curteisie courteous conduct
48	therto moreover
	ferre further
49	As wel ... hethenesse as much in Christian as in non-Christian lands
51	Alisaundre Alexandria (Egypt), taken in 1365 by Christian knights under Peter of Lusignan, King of Cyprus and sixth Latin king of Jerusalem

Lines 43–78 The Knight continued

CHECK THE BOOK
Consult a large modern European atlas and see how many of these places you can find.

	GLOSSARY
52	**Ful ... bigonne** many a time had he taken the head of the table (the place of honour)
53	**Pruce** Prussia, seat of the Teutonic Knights
54	**Lettow** Lithuania, which followed its Prince Jagiello into the Catholic Church in 1386
	reysed campaigned
	Ruce Russia
55	**degree** rank
56	**Gernade** Granada, the Moorish province in southern Spain
57	**Algezir** Algeciras, taken in 1344, whereafter the Benmarin dynasty returned to their kingdom in Southern Morocco (Belmarye), where Christian knights also campaigned
58	**Lyeys** Ayas, Armenian port near Antioch, in modern Turkey
	Satalye Attalia, in Armenia
59	**Whan** when (Peter of Cyprus took them in 1367 and 1361 respectively)
	Grete See Mediterranean
60	**armee** military expedition
62	**oure feith** Christianity
	Tramyssene Tlemçen, Western Algeria
63	**lystes** in a tournament or formal combat of champions
	ay always
65	**Palatye** Balat in modern Turkey (ancient Miletus). An emir of Balat was a vassal of Peter of Cyprus
66	**Agayn** against
67	**And ... prys** and always he had an outstanding reputation
68	**worthy** brave
	wys wise, discreet
69	**port** bearing
70	**vileynye** rudeness
71	**maner wight** kind of person
72	**verray** true (*not* very)
	parfit complete
	gentil noble
74	**His hors ... gay** his horses were good, but he was not gaily dressed himself
75	**fustian** coarse cotton cloth
	gypon tunic

GLOSSARY

76	**bismotered** marked, spotted (with rust)
	habergeon hauberk, coat of mail
77	**late** recently
	viage campaign

LINES 79–100 THE SQUIRE

The Knight's son is an Esquire, or candidate for knighthood; an apprentice knight in the service of a senior knight. He has fought well, across the English Channel. He is a *lovyere*, full of youth, gaiety and the qualities of spring. He also has all the courtly accomplishments and treats his father with honour.

QUESTION
Compare the motives, enemies, and dress of father and son. For whose sake does each perform his feats of war? (see **Characterisation, The Military**).

GLOSSARY

80	**lovyere** lover
	lusty zestful (*not* lustful)
	bacheler probationer for the honour of knighthood (the candidate had to win his spurs by passing military and religious tests)
81	**lokkes ... presse** locks as curly as if they had been in curlers
83	**of evene lengthe** well-proportioned
84	**delyvere** agile
85	**chyvachie** cavalry expedition
86	**In ... Pycardie** in Flanders, in Artois and Picardy. These parts of modern France and Belgium across the Channel from Kent were provinces claimed by England in its Hundred Years War which had begun in 1338. Chaucer had fought in France in 1359
87	**And ... space** and conducted himself so well in such a short time
89	**Embrouded** embroidered (of his clothing)
	meede meadow
91	**floytynge** playing the flute
94	**koude** knew how to
95	**endite** compose words to songs
96	**Juste** joust in a tournament
	purtreye portray, draw

GLOSSARY

97	hoote hotly
	nyghtertale night-time
98	sleep slept
	nyghtyngale the bird of love (compare line 11)
100	carf carved (the meat): one of the duties of an Esquire

LINES 101–17 THE YEOMAN

CONTEXT

Chaucer's Yeoman is the basis of Walter Scott's description of Robin Hood in his prose romance, *Ivanhoe*, 1819.

The Knight's only follower is a yeoman, a word which in the next century came to mean a small landholder. The Knight's yeoman was obliged to follow the Knight to war. He is a forester by calling, as his *takel* shows, and had perhaps been an archer in the French wars; his six-foot longbow had a range of 265 metres. He wears a medal of St Christopher, the patron saint of foresters.

The Yeoman is picturesque but anonymous, as are his lord and his lord's son. Are the military trio individuals or types or ideals? If ideals, ideals of what? What unites them and what divides them? (see **Characterisation, The Military**).

GLOSSARY

102	hym liste it pleased him
103	he the yeoman
104	pecok peacock; the arrow was trimmed with peacock feathers to guide its flight
107	His arwes ... lowe his arrows did not fall short with sagging feathers
109	not heed close-cropped head
111	bracer archer's arm-guard
112	bokeler buckler, shield
114	Harneised ornamented
116	bawdryk baldric, belt

LINES 118–62 THE PRIORESS

The Prioress is a lady as well as a nun, and models her manners on those of court. To keep little dogs was forbidden by the rules of some convents.

For a discussion of her portrait, see **Extended commentaries, text 2**.

GLOSSARY

118	Nonne nun, a woman who takes solemn religious vows
119	symple and coy shy and quiet
120	ooth oath
	but only
	Loy Eloi, Eligius, a founder of convents; also patron saint of goldsmiths
121	Eglentyne (French) sweetbriar. A name from romances
122	service dyvyne divine worship (the regular church liturgy)
123	Entuned intoned
	semely becomingly
124	fetisly gracefully
125	Stratford not Stratford-upon-Avon but Stratford, Bromley by Bow, Middlesex, where there was a Benedictine convent known to Chaucer. The Prioress's French was not Parisian, though this may not be a criticism
127	At mete at table (not meat)
	with alle indeed
130	kepe take care
132	In ... lest she took a particular pleasure in courtly behaviour
134	coppe cup
	ferthyng spot the size of a farthing coin; a farthing is the fourth part of a penny
136	after ... raughte reached for her food
137	sikerly certainly
	greet desport fine deportment
138	of port in her bearing
139	peyned hire took pains
	countrefete cheere imitate the manner
140	estatlich dignified

Lines 118–62 The Prioress continued

GLOSSARY

141	**to ben … reverence** to be esteemed worthy of respect
142	**for to speken** to speak
	conscience conscience; also, sensibility
143	**pitous** pitying, soft-hearted
145	**bledde** was bleeding
146	**Of smale houndes** some little dogs
147	**flessh** meat
	wastel-breed cake (French *gâteau*), or fine bread
148	**soore** sorely
	oon one
149	**men** someone (an impersonal construction, as with 'one')
	with a yerde smerte sharply with a stick
151	**wympul** wimple, a nun's prescribed neck-covering
	pynched pleated
152	**tretys** well formed
153	**thereto** moreover
154	**sikerly** indeed
155	**spanne** stretch between little finger and thumb
156	**hardily** scarcely
157	**fetys** well made
	was war noticed
158	**smal** slender
159	**peire of bedes** set of beads, used for saying the Rosary, a sequence of prayers to the Virgin Mary
	gauded embellished
160	**sheene** beautiful
161	**write** engraved, cut
	crowned A a capital A (for Latin *Amor*, or for Richard II's queen, Anne
162	**'*Amor vincit omnia*'** 'Love conquers all' (secular) or 'Love binds all' (religious)
164	**chapeleyne** assistant (*not* chaplain)

LINES 165–207 THE MONK

The senior male cleric present is a Benedictine monk, whose religious vows were the same as those of the Nun, though he takes a more relaxed view of them. Monks were often caricatured as too fond of hunting and good living.

Chaucer says (line 183) that he said that the Monk's opinion was good. How can we tell that it is not good? How does Chaucer know that the Monk liked roast swan better than other roasts? What impression does the Monk seek to create by his dress and talk? What impression does he actually make? By what means does Chaucer suggest the difference? (see **Characterisation, The Clergy**).

CONTEXT

The Rule of St Benedict (or Benet) of Norcia (480–550) was the foundation of Western monasticism.

GLOSSARY

165	**a fair for the maistrie** a surpassingly fine one
166	**outridere** rider-out, estate supervisor
	venerie hunting
167	**to been … able** worthy to have been head of an abbey
168	**deyntee** fine
170	**Gynglen** to jingle (bells on the bridle were popular, especially with Canterbury pilgrims)
172	**Ther … celle** where this lord [a monk was addressed as lord or *daun*, from Latin *dominus*] was in charge of the house
173	**reule** monastic Rule. St Maurus was Benedict's disciple
174	**somdel streit** rather strict
175	**ilke** same
	leet … pace allowed old things [such as Rules] to pass away
176	**heeld … space** observed the freedom of modern times
177	**yaf** gave
	pulled hen plucked hen (a worthless object)
178	**hunters … men** a traditional comment on hunters in the Bible, such as Esau
179	**recchelees** careless (of his duty)
180	**waterlees** out of water. ('A monk out of his monastery is like a fish out of water.' Benedictines take a vow of 'stability' to their own monastery)
181	**cloystre** cloister, monastery

Lines 165–207 The Monk continued

CONTEXT

One can learn much about St Thomas, and the pilgrimage, at Canterbury Cathedral museum, which has some paintings of Chaucer's pilgrims.

GLOSSARY

184	**What** why
	wood mad
185	**poure** stare
186	**swynken** toil
187	**Austyn** St Augustine of Hippo (354–430), Doctor of the Church, who **bit** (bid, commanded) that the religious should do manual work
	served served, serviced; clerics were sometimes administrators in the world
188	**Lat Austyn … reserved!** let Austin keep his hard work to himself
189	**he** the Monk
	prikasour mounted hunter who follows the hare by its pawprints or 'pricks'
192	**lust** pleasure
	cost expense
193	**seigh** saw
	purfiled trimmed at the edge
194	**grys** a grey squirrel fur
195	**festne** fasten
196	**ywroght** wrought, made
	curious remarkable
197	**love-knotte** device
	gretter larger
198	**balled** bald
199	**as … enoynt** as if he had been anointed (which, if he is also a priest, he would have been)
200	**poynt** physical condition
201	**stepe** prominent
	heed head
202	**stemed as … leed** gleamed like the fire under a cauldron
204	**prelaat** senior cleric
205	**forpyned** wasted by suffering
206	**roost** roast meat (monks were forbidden to eat quadrupeds)
207	**palfrey** horse
	berye berry

LINES 208–69 THE FRIAR

A Friar (Latin *frater*, French *frère*, brother) though a member of a religious community is not bound to a monastic life of prayer, but preaches the gospel in the world, living off charity. A friar is not a monk. Friars were accused of abusing the freedom given them as mendicants (beggars) and travellers, and were satirised for the faults exemplified in this portrait.

This is the longest portrait. Anti-fraternal satire (i.e., against friars), mostly written by clerics, expresses disgust at the way the friars, masters of the arts of preaching, could use them for begging. But Chaucer praises his social skill and charm, his preference for eating with the rich rather than feeding the poor.

What use does Chaucer make of anticlimax in this portrait? (see **Characterisation, The Clergy**).

> **QUESTION**
> What is the effect of phrases such as *as seyde himself* and *he dorste make avaunt?*

GLOSSARY

208	**wantowne** lively
210	**ordres foure** (i) the Franciscans or Friars Minor, founded by St Francis of Assisi in 1210, known as the Grey Friars; (ii) the Dominicans, or Order of Preachers, founded by St Dominic in 1216, known as the Black Friars; (iii) the Carmelites, or White Friars; (iv) the Austin Friars (see note on line 187)
209	**lymytour** one licensed to beg in a limited district
	solempne imposing
210	**kan** knows
211	**daliaunce** flirtatious flattery
212	**maad** arranged
213	**cost** expense
214	**post** pillar, support (see Galatians 2:9, where apostles are 'pillars' of the Church). Possibly the young women had to get married because they were pregnant by this *noble post*
215	**famulier** intimate
216	**frankeleyns** franklins, householders who were often prosperous and hospitable (see lines 331–60)
	over above
	contree district

Lines 208–69 The Friar continued

Since the previous century, every Christian had been required to confess his sins once a year privately to a priest.

GLOSSARY

217 worthy prosperous

218 confessioun the Sacrament of Confession, or Penance. If truly contrite, the penitent is absolved of the guilt of his sins. The Friar claims to have been empowered to absolve certain sins that the *curat* (line 219), a secular priest, had to refer to his bishop for absolution

220 licenciat licensed to hear confessions

224 Ther as in cases where

wiste hoped

pitaunce charitable donation

225 povre poor; all four Orders were vowed to poverty

226 yshryve shriven, absolved of sin

227 he the penitent

He … avaunt the friar dared assert

228 He wiste he knew

repentaunt (repentance is prerequisite to absolution)

230 He … smerte he is not able to weep (the Friar suggests), although he is deeply pained. (The sincere penitent was expected to weep. The Friar accepts money instead)

231 preyeres prayers (imposed as a penance)

232 moote are permitted

233 typet … farsed cape was always stuffed

234 wyves women

235 murye note merry singing voice

236 koude knew how to

rote stringed instrument

237 yeddynges ballad romances

baar … pris took the prize outright

238 flour-de-lys lily

241 hostiler innkeeper

tappestere a female tapster, barmaid

242 Bet better

lazar leper (after Lazarus)

beggestere beggar-woman (the kind of person friars should help)

244 Acorded suited

facultee official position

GLOSSARY

246	honest respectable
	avaunce be advantageous
247	swich poraille such a poor class of people
248	riche rich people
	vitaille victuals, food
249	over above
	ther as wherever
250	lowely of servyse humble in offering his services
252a	ferme rent
	graunt licence (to beg in that district)
252b	haunt home territory
253	sho shoe (a worthless object)
	'In principio' (Latin) 'in the beginning' (the opening words of St John's Gospel, and a favourite greeting of mendicant friars)
255	ferthyng farthing, the fourth part of a penny
	er before
256	His purchas ... rente his pickings were much better than his official income
257	And rage ... whelp he knew how to play, just as if he were a pup
258	love-dayes days fixed for settling disputes out of court, often by the arbitration of the clergy, who sometimes abused their powers
259	cloysterer one who lives in a cloister (like a monk, as opposed to one who lives in the world)
260	cope a priest's vestment
	scoler student (like the Clerk in line 290)
261	maister Master of Arts, a dignified title, like the modern Doctor of Divinity
	pope the Pope, head of the Church
262	double worstede extra-thick woven woollen cloth
	semycope a short cape
263	rounded ... presse curved out like a bell from the mould (in the bell foundry)
264	lipsed lisped
	wantownesse self-indulgence

CONTEXT

A penance is a token punishment for sin awarded after confession, as a condition of absolution. Medieval penances were often physical: a pilgrimage was a common form of penance.

LINES 270–84 THE MERCHANT

The Merchant is neither a soldier nor a cleric, and comes first in the third estate, that of the workers, many of whom have mercantile values. He may be a member of the Merchants Adventurers or the Merchants of the Staple, the merchant guilds of the City of London who ran the trade between England and the Low Countries, especially the export of English cloth – a trade with which Chaucer would have to do when he worked as a customs officer. City merchants were regarded with suspicion, especially if they traded in money as well as goods.

The substantial Merchant impresses and mystifies Chaucer with his talk of his profits, his foreign exchange dealings and the importance of protecting shipping routes. Are we to be impressed? Is it significant that Chaucer is not able to discover his name? (see **Characterisation, Professionals**).

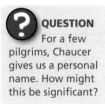

QUESTION
For a few pilgrims, Chaucer gives us a personal name. How might this be significant?

GLOSSARY

276	**He wolde … any thyng** he wanted the sea to be guarded against all hazards
277	**Middelburgh** the Staple port on the island of Walcheren in the Netherlands; across the North Sea from Orwell, near Ipswich, Suffolk, where Chaucer's family came from
278	**sheeldes** *écus*, French coins with a *shield* on one side. The Merchant traded in currency, which the Church considered tantamount to usury
279	**bisette** employed
280	**wiste** knew
	wight creature
281	**estatly** dignified
	governaunce conduct
282	**chevyssaunce** borrowing money
283	**For sothe** forsooth, truly
	with alle after all
284	**noot** know not

LINES 285–308 THE CLERK

The Clerk is a model university student, reading for a career in the Church. He is in minor orders.

Chaucer writes approvingly of the Clerk's books and conversation, but makes a joke about the unprofitability of philosophy. Can we draw any conclusions from this? What are the points of comparison with the Merchant's portrait? (see **Characterisation, Professionals**).

CONTEXT

The modern word clerk comes from Latin *Clericus*. The clergy supplied nearly all the earlier writers of the Middle Ages.

GLOSSARY

285	**Oxenford** Oxford, seat of a university since the twelfth century
286	**logyk** logic, the principal subject in Arts
	ygo gone, applied
287	**leene** lean
288	**And he … undertake** and the clerk himself was not very fat, I swear

CONTEXT

Aristotle was a Greek philosopher (384–322 BC) whose works, preserved and interpreted by Christian and Arabic philosophers, revolutionised Western philosophy when in the twelfth century they reached Paris from Moorish Spain.

GLOSSARY

289	holwe hollow
	sobrely gravely
290	overeste topmost
	courtepy short cape
291	geten hym got himself
	benefice living, post as a parish priest
292	office secular employment (usually administrative)
293	hym … have he would rather have
	heed side
294	Twenty a large number of manuscript volumes
294	blak or reed calf or sheepskin
296	or fithele, or gay sautrie fiddles and psalteries were popular with students
297	philosophre (i) philosopher or natural scientist, hence (ii) alchemist, seeker after the fabulous philosopher's stone which turned base metal into gold. A play on both senses of the word
298	cofre chest
299	hente obtain. Students often had to beg for support
301	bisily earnestly
	gan began
302	hem … scoleye those who gave him the means to study
303	cure care
304	o one
	neede needful
305	forme due form
306	quyk lively, sharp
	hy sentence elevated content
307	Sownynge in tending to (compare line 275)

LINES 309–30 THE SERGEANT OF THE LAW

Sergeants-at-Law (*servientes ad legem*) were the king's servants in legal matters, chosen from among the senior barristers. Those of them who were not judges could act as circuit judges, like Chaucer's Sergeant, but still pleaded in the courts and could grow rich on their fees. They were criticised for their purchase of lands previously given by the king for services rendered.

One of these Sergeants was Thomas Pynchbec, who in 1388 signed a warrant for the arrest of Chaucer for debt. The possible pun in line 326 has suggested him as a source of this portrait.

Compare the learning and conversation of the Clerk with those of the Sergeant, and the uses to which they are put. Examine the implications of lines 313, 320 and 326 (see **Characterisation, Professionals**).

GLOSSARY

309	**war** cautious
310	**Parvys** Paradise, a name for the covered portico of a church, especially that of St Paul's, the cathedral of the City of London, the traditional meeting-place for lawyers and their clients
311	**of** in
313	**He semed ... so wise** he seemed to be so, for his words were so wise
314	**Justice** judge
	assise assize or sitting of a court, held periodically in each county before judge and jury
315	**patente** patent, an open letter from the king
	pleyn commissioun commission giving full powers
316	**science** knowledge
	renoun reputation
317	**robes** given by clients in addition to their fees
	many oon many a one
318	**purchasour** buyer-up of land
319	**fee symple** unrestricted ownership in law
	In effect in the end result
320	**infect** invalidated (he made sure that his legal entitlement to any land he purchased was proof against legal challenge)
321	**nas** was not
323	**In termes** in exact legal terms
	caas cases. English common law is 'case law', based on preceding decisions in similar cases
	doomes decisions

CONTEXT

After the Norman Conquest the language of English administration and law was French. Parliament was first opened in English instead of French in 1362.

GLOSSARY

324	**William** William the Conqueror, the Norman duke who conquered England in 1066.
	were falle had occurred
325	**endite** write
	make a thyng draw up a deed
326	**pynche** pick holes in, find fault with
327	**statut** statute, Act of Parliament
	koude knew
	pleyn by rote completely by heart
328	**He ... hoomly** the dress in which he rode was plain
	medlee of mixed weave
329	**ceint** belt
329	**barres smalle** narrow stripes
330	**telle I no lenger tale** I say no more

LINES 331–60 THE FRANKLIN

CONTEXT
The four humours (hot, cold, moist and dry), themselves combinations of the four elements (earth, air, fire and water), produced four complexions (line 335, melancholy, choleric, phlegmatic and sanguine). In medieval medicine, blood predominated in a *sangwyn* complexion: ruddy of face, pleasure-loving, of good digestion and humour.

A Franklin was a country gentleman, a free man who held land direct from the Crown, without a knight's obligation to military service.

For a discussion of this portrait, see **Characterisation, Professionals** and **Extended commentaries, text 3,** where there is also a translation. The nature of true felicity or happiness was a question of moral philosophy which interested Chaucer. The Franklin is amusingly self-indulgent, but before we condemn him we should remember that Chaucer had been a JP and an MP, that his family were vintners (line 342), and that he presents himself as large in the waist.

GLOSSARY

332	**dayesye** daisy (literally 'day's eye'), a flower Chaucer often mentions
333	**complexioun** not facial colour but temperament or combination of 'humours', which produced it.
334	**by the morwe** in the morning
	a sop in wyn a piece of cake dipped in wine (a common light breakfast)

GLOSSARY

335 **wone** custom

336 **Epicurus** the austere Athenian Philosopher (341–270BC), who held that pleasure, or the absence of pain, was the chief good. His 'Sons', the Epicureans, were later supposed to be gourmets or epicures

337 **pleyn delit** complete pleasure

338 **verray felicitee parfit** true and perfect happiness

340 **Julian** Julian the Hospitaller, a legendary saint famed for his hospitality

contree part of the world

341 **after oon** of one standard (the best)

342 **bettre envyned** with a better cellar

343 **mete** food

344 **flessh** meat

plentevous plenteous

345 **snewed** snowed

347 **After** according to

349 **partrich** partridge

muwe cage

350 **breem** bream

luce pike

stuwe fish-pond (*not* stew)

351 **Wo was** unhappy was

but if unless

352 **Poynaunt** piquant

geere utensils for the table

353 **table dormant** a fixed table for hospitality (most tables were trestle)

354 **al … day** all day long

355 **At sessions … lord and sire** he presided over the sessions of the county court (as a Justice of the Peace; see line 314)

356 **knyght of the shire** Member of Parliament for the county

357 **anlaas** dagger

gipser purse

358 **Heeng** hung

morne morning

CONTEXT

Chaucer casually mentions Aristotle, Epicurus, and, later, Plato. The old idea that medieval people were ignorant of classical learning is questionable.

> **GLOSSARY**
>
> 359   **shirreve** sheriff, the king's steward (reeve) in a county (shire); the most important office after the lord lieutenant of a county
>
>   **contour** auditor of county finances
>
> 360   **vavasour** large landholder (vassal's vassal)

LINES 361–78 THE FIVE GUILDSMEN

As the five tradesmen each have a different craft, the guild whose livery they wear here must be religious. Guilds were the organisms of social life in medieval cities; their property was confiscated under Edward VI in the sixteenth century, much as his father, Henry VIII, had taken the property of the monks in the 1530s.

By what means does Chaucer manage to suggest the Guildsmen's corporate estimate of themselves? (see **Characterisation, Professionals**).

CONTEXT

A guild was originally the fraternity of a trade or craft, but by the fourteenth century there were also religious and social guilds.

> **GLOSSARY**
>
> 361   **haberdasshere** retailer of small articles of dress
>
> 362   **webbe** weaver
>
>   **dyere** dyer of cloth
>
>   **tapycer** tapestry-maker
>
> 363   **o lyveree** the same livery or uniform
>
> 364   **greet** important
>
> 365   **geere** gear
>
>   **apiked** picked out, trimmed
>
> 366   **chaped** mounted (silver mountings were permitted by law to tradesmen of property worth £500 or more)
>
> 367   **wroght** made
>
> 368   **everydeel** in every way
>
> 369   **burgeys** burgess, established citizen
>
> 370   **yeldehalle** guildhall, seat of city government
>
>   **deys** dais, platform
>
>   **everich** each
>
>   **kan** knows

GLOSSARY

372	**shaply suited**
	alderman civic officer assisting the mayor
373	**catel** property
	rente income
374	**assente** testify (to their wealth)
375	**elles** otherwise
	to blame blameworthy
376	**ycleped** called
377	**And goon ... bifore** and go to vigils in front of everyone. On vigils, the eves of feast days, the guild would go to its chapel (compare lines 449–50)
378	**roialliche ybore** royally carried for you (by a servant)

LINES 379–87 THE COOK

The Cook, retained by the guildsmen for the pilgrimage as an indication of their importance, is not a very good cook, to judge by his repertoire and his ulcer. (He tells a vulgar tale and falls off his horse at the end of the pilgrimage, drunk.)

Is the *mormal* of line 386 significant? (see **Characterisation, Professionals**).

QUESTION
Chaucer openly criticises only his social inferiors among the pilgrims, beginning with the Cook. Is this the voice of Chaucer the pilgrim or of the poet?

GLOSSARY

379	**for the nones** for the occasion
380	**marybones** marrow bones
381	**poudre-marchant** flavouring powder
	tart tart, sharp-tasting
	galyngale sweet cyperus root, a spice like ginger
382	**Wel ... knowe** he knew well how to assess
	Londoun ale considered the best
383	**koude ... sethe** knew how to roast and boil
384	**mortreux** a stew, the elements of which were prepared in a mortar
	pye pie

GLOSSARY

385	**thoughte me** seemed to me
386	**shyne** shin
	mormal a dried-up ulcer
387	**For** as for
	blankmanger a mousse, of minced capon boiled in milk and sugar (*not* blancmange)
	with equal to

LINES 388–410 THE SHIPMAN

The Shipman is the master of his barge, the *Maudelayne*. Dartmouth, 200 miles from London on the south coast of Devon, was a big port. The Bordeaux trade was the heart of the wine trade, Chaucer's family's business. As a customs officer, he knew about shipmen, who do not appear in other works satirising social types.

To what ends does this pilgrim devote his superlative professional skill? What is the effect of placing *ydrawe* at the end of line 396? Would we answer differently if we did not know something about Chaucer's own background? (see **Characterisation, Professionals**).

CONTEXT

Chaucer's father and grandfather were wine-mechants, and he worked for a time in the office of Customs.

GLOSSARY

388	**wonynge … weste** dwelling far to the west
389	**woot** know
390	**roucny** a powerful horse; or, possibly, a nag
	as he kouthe as he knew how (that is, poorly)
391	**faldyng** coarse woollen cloth
392	**laas** lace, cord (like the lanyard of the Royal Navy)
395	**felawe** companion
396	**ydrawe** (i) carried as cargo, (ii) stolen secretly
397	**Fro Burdeux-ward** coming from Bordeaux (the wine port of Aquitaine, formerly an English possession)
	chapman merchant
398	**nyce** delicate
	keep notice (compare the Prioress, line 142)

GLOSSARY

399	**faught** fought (with pirates)
	hyer hond upper hand, victory
400	**sent … hoom** a common practice: he drowned his prisoners
401	**craft** skill (*not* ship)
402	**hym bisides** which affected him
403	**herberwe** harbour
	lodemenage pilotage. (The 'lodestar' is the North Star, which 'leads' navigators)
404	**noon swich** none like him
	Hulle port in the north-east of England
	Cartage either Carthage, a landmark on the N.African coast, or Cartagena, the Spanish port
405	**Hardy** tough
	wys to undertake prudent in an undertaking
408	**Gootlond** Gotland; the Baltic island with its port, Visby
	Fynystere Finisterra, Spain (*not* Finisterre, Brittany)
409	**cryke** creek, harbour
	Britaigne Brittany (*not* Britain)
410	**Maudelayne** a vessel of this name is recorded in Dartmouth in 1379 and in 1391, when its master was a Peter Risshenden. A barge was a trading vessel of between 100 and 200 tons

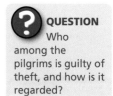

QUESTION
Who among the pilgrims is guilty of theft, and how is it regarded?

LINES 411–44 THE DOCTOR OF PHYSIC

Doctors came low on the social scale. The Physician is, even more than most of the pilgrims, a master of his art. Medicine then included other sciences such as astrology which now seem unscientific to modern Western medicine. His authorities are the ancient and the Arabic doctors.

Is there any conclusion to be drawn from the disparity between the Doctor's immense learning and the final end to which it is put? (consider lines 441–44, and see **Characterisation – Professionals**).

Lines 411–44 The Doctor of Physic continued

GLOSSARY

413	To speke of if we consider
414	astronomye astrology
415	kepte watched
	deel deal (of time)
416	In houres at the astronomical hours of planetary influences upon the patient
	magyk natureel astrology (which dealt with the 'natural' heavenly bodies, not with spirits, as did black magic)
417	Wel … ascendent he knew well how to find the Ascendent in favourable position (The Ascendent is the Zodiacal sign rising above the eastern horizon; whether or not it is 'fortunate' depends upon the conjunction of the planets, which the Doctor foresees)
418	ymages talismans associated with Zodiacal signs
419	everich maladye every illness
	Were it … drye see note to complexioun, line 333
422	praktisour practitioner
423	The cause … roote once the cause was known and the source of his disease
424	Anon … boote he at once gave the sick man his remedy
426	drogges drugs
	letuaries medical syrups
427	For … wynne for each of them made the other to gain
428	newe to bigynne newly begun
429–34	Esculapius legendary father of medicine, Aesculapius, a Greek god, supposed in the Middle Ages to be the author of several books. Fourteen medical authorities follow, Greek, Arab and modern.
432	Serapion Arab writer of the eleventh century
	Razis Rhazes (of Baghdad)
	Avycen Avicenna (of Bokhara)
433	Averrois Averroes (of Cordoba) – all were famous Muslim philosophers of the eleventh and twelfth centuries
433	Damascien may refer to the writings of two authors
	Constantyn monk of Carthage who brought Middle Eastern learning to Salerno in the eleventh century
434	Bernard, Gatesden, Gilbertyn modern British trio: Bernard Gordon, a Scot, Professor of Medicine at Montpellier about 1300; John of Gaddesden of Merton College, Oxford, who died in 1361; Gilbertus Anglicus lived in the thirteenth century

CONTEXT

Medical authorities: Dioscorides wrote in the first century AD, Rufus in the second, as did Galen, the great medical authority of antiquity. Hippocrates, the founder of Greek medical science, flourished in the fifth century BC. Haly may be the Persian Hali ibn el Abbas (died 994)

GLOSSARY

438	**His studie … Bible** Doctors are often charged with materialism
439	**sangwyn** red cloth
	pers a Persian blue-grey cloth
440	**taffata** taffeta
	sendal a thin silk
441	**esy of dispence** slow to spend money
442	**that** what
	pestilence plague-time. The Black Death of 1349, which killed a third of the population of England, was the worst of four major outbreaks of bubonic plague in Chaucer's day
443	**For** as
	cordial medicine for heart; gold indeed formed part of prescriptions, but the next line is another comment on the doctor's avarice

LINES 445–76 THE WIFE OF BATH

The Wife comes from the cloth-making neighbourhood of Bath, and is, like other pilgrims, skilful in her profession. As the widow of a guildsman, she could have an independent practice. 'Wife' means 'woman' not 'married woman', but she has married five times, and, as she says in the Prologue to her tale, she would welcome a sixth husband.

In interpreting such details as the Wife's teeth or hat and spurs, medieval physiognomy and astrology are helpful (see **Characterisation, Professionals and Good Men**). But an awareness of medieval doctrines on the place of woman is not needed to see why the Wife loves the package-tour aspect of pilgrimages.

 CHECK THE BOOK

The Wife's five husbands invite a comparison with the Samaritan woman with five husbands whose meeting with Jesus is recounted in St John's Gospel 4:17.

GLOSSARY

445	**biside** nearby. The parish of St Michael's-juxta-Bathon was a centre of cloth-making. The weaving trade made parts of the West Country and the Cotswolds rich
446	**somdel deef** somewhat deaf – as the result of a blow on the ear from her fifth husband, as recounted in the Wife's own Prologue

Lines 445–76 The Wife of Bath continued

The Offertory. Today money is collected, but medieval people processed up to the altar in order of social precedence (see line 377) with gifts of their own manufacture.

GLOSSARY	
446	**scathe** a pity
447	**haunt** skill
448	**passed** surpassed
448	**Gaunt** Ghent; like Ypres, a centre of Flemish weaving. Edward III attracted many Flemish weavers to settle in England, improving the weaving of English wool
449	**In al the parisshe … noon** not a woman in the whole parish
450	**offrynge** Offertory, the part of the Mass when the people offer gifts.
	bifore in front of
451	**ther dide** any woman were to do so
	wrooth angry
452	**out of alle charitee** beyond thought of being charitable; angry
453	**coverchiefs** head-coverings
	fyne … of ground finely woven
454	**weyeden ten pound** weighed ten pounds (nearly 5 kilos)
456	**hosen** stockings (The Wife uses the Offertory procession as a shop window for her wares, and for herself)
457	**streite** tightly
	moyste soft
	fair pleasing
	hewe hue
459	**lyve** life
460	**at chirche dore** in front of the church door (where all marriages took place)
	fyve the number of husbands of the Samaritan woman in the Gospel
461	**Withouten** not counting
	oother compaignye a hint at promiscuity
462	**nedeth nat** it is not necessary
	as nowthe for the present, just now
463	**Jerusalem** (pronounced 'Jersalem'). Pilgrimages to the Holy Land were not uncommon, although in going thrice (**thries**) the Wife is characteristically excessive
464	**straunge strem** foreign river
465	**Rome** where Saints Peter and Paul were martyred
	Boloigne Boulogne-sur-Mer boasted a miraculous image of the Virgin Mary

GLOSSARY

466	**Galice at Seint-Jame** the very popular shrine of St James the Greater, at Compostella, Galicia, northwest Spain
	Coloigne Cologne in Germany housed the shrine of the Three Kings and of St Ursula
467	**She koude … weye** she knew a lot about wandering along, or off, the road. (Compare the 'straight and narrow way' of Matthew 7:14)
468	**Gat-tothed** gate-toothed, with teeth widely spaced. The Wife in her Prologue associates this with Venus
469	**amblere** an ambling horse
	esily in a relaxed way
	sat she rides astride in the Ellesmere MS illustration. (Riding side-saddle was introduced into England by Anne of Bohemia, Richard II's first wife)
470	**Ywympled wel** with a large wimple
471	**bokeler or a targe** buckler or a shield
472	**foot-mantel** a riding-skirt, or outer skirt
	large ample (the skirt, not the hips)
473	**spores** spurs
474	**felaweshipe** company
	carpe talk
476	**the olde daunce** (proverbial phrase) like 'all the ins and outs'

LINES 477–528 THE PARSON

The Parson is the ideal parish priest, free from the faults both of the regular clergy already described and of some parish priests. He cares for his flock rather than himself, and is free from the hypocrisy and greed of some of the pilgrims.

Which details of his portrait back up the claim made in its last line? (see **Characterisation, Good Men**).

QUESTION
Why is the Parson described in terms of his virtues rather than his tastes, physique or dress?

GLOSSARY

478	**toun** village
482	**parisshens** parishioners, inhabitants of his parish

Lines 477–528 The Parson continued

CONTEXT

Tithe (from 'tenth')
(line 486): Laymen
were obliged to
give one-tenth of
their income or
produce to support
their priest. Non-
payment could
mean exclusion
from the
sacrament of
communion.
Agricultural
produce was
gathered into
Tithe Barns, some
of which survive
today.

CONTEXT

A chantry was a
provision for a
priest to say (or
chant) a daily mass
for the repose of
the soul of a
deceased person –
an easier life than
that of a country
parish.

GLOSSARY

483	**Benygne** gracious
485	**ypreved ... sithes** often proven
486	**Ful looth ... tithes** he was very reluctant to excommunicate for his tithes.
487	**But ... out of doute** but, beyond doubt, he would rather give
488	**aboute** in the parish
489	**offryng** money given at the Offertory (see line 450) at Easter supports the priest
	substaunce property
490	**koude** knew how to (*see* Christian comedy – *truth*)
491	**fer asonder** far apart
493	**meschief** misfortune
494	**muche and lite** great and small
495	**Upon ... a staf** according to the example of early Christian pastors
498	**gospel** Matthew 5:19
499	**figure** analogy
500	**That ... do** traditional image
502	**lewed** unlearned
	ruste rust, tarnish
503	**keep** notice
504	**shiten** covered in excrement
505	**Wel ... yive** it well becomes a priest to set an example
507	**sette ... hire** did not rent out his living. Absentee parsons appointed vicars and curates
508	**And leet ... myre** nor left his sheep (people) stuck in the bog (of sin)
	To seken ... soules to get himself a chantry for souls.
511	**Or ... withholde** or to be retained by a guild (as chaplain)
512	**kepte ... folde** kept watch over his sheepfold
513	**myscarie** come to destruction
514	**mercenarie** hireling. From the parable in John's Gospel 10:12. The wolf represents the Devil
516	**despitous** contemptuous
517	**daungerous ne digne** arrogant nor haughty
518	**discreet** courteous
519	**fairnesse** attraction

GLOSSARY

520	his bisynesse what he worked for
521	But unless
522	What so whatever
	lough estat low position
523	snybben rebuke
	for the nonys for that reason
524	trowe believe
	nowher noon ys is none anywhere
525	He ... reverence he expected no reverence
526	spiced over-scrupulous
527	loore teaching
	apostles twelve i.e., their example
528	He taughte ... hymselve the parson practised what he preached

LINES 529–41 THE PLOUGHMAN

The Ploughman is as virtuous as his brother the Parson. He is a hard worker who loves God and his neighbour, serves others and pays his tithes. Although a peasant, the Ploughman is a small tenant farmer and a free man; not a serf bonded to stay on his manor.

Why are Parson and Ploughman brothers? What are the points of contrast between them and the pilgrims who precede them? (see **Characterisation, Good Men**).

CHECK THE BOOK

Piers Plowman, by Chaucer's contemporary William Langland, is a dream-vision of a Plowman: the archetypal medieval man.

GLOSSARY

529	was 'he' is understood
530	ylad ... fother pulled many a cart-load of dung
531	A trewe ... was he he was a good hard worker. (Compare the modern English 'a good man and true')
532	charitee the supreme theological virtue, defined in the next lines in the words of Christ's supreme commandment
533	hoole whole
534	thogh ... smerte whether it was pleasant or painful to him
536	and ... delve and also dig ditches and make hedges

Lines 529–41 The Ploughman continued

CHECK THE NET
Suggestions for further critical reading can be found at http://www.courses.fas.harvard.edu/~chaucer/

GLOSSARY

537	**povre wight** poor creature
538	**hire** payment
	myght power
539	**tithes** tenth part of a man's produce, due to the Church
540	**propre swynk** own labour (that is, the corn from the fields he ploughed)
	catel property, possessions (*not* cows)
541	**mere** mare (regarded as an inferior mount)
542	**reve** Reeve, estate-manager
544	**somnour** Summoner (to the church court)
	pardoner supplier of Pardons or Indulgences
544	**maunciple** Manciple, college servant
	namo no more

LINES 545–66 THE MILLER

The Miller leads the rascally final group of pilgrims. A mill had the monopoly of grinding all the corn on a manor, and could charge a high price. This miller was strong and quarrelsome, which made it easier for him to abuse his monopoly.

The vices of the previous pilgrims were not obvious, nor were they criticised openly. Does the method of presentation begin to change now? What are the common elements in the similes in this portrait? (see **Characterisation, Stewards**).

GLOSSARY

545	**stout** sturdy
	carl churl, fellow
	for the nones indeed
547	**proved** was shown
	over al everywhere
	ther he cam where he went
548	**ram** the prize in a wrestling match
549	**short-sholdred** broad-shouldered

GLOSSARY

	knarre knot
550	Ther ... harre there was no door that he could not heave off its hinge
551	at a rennyng with a single charge
552	berd beard
	reed red
554	Upon ... right right on the top of
555	werte wart
	toft of herys tuft of hairs
556	brustles bristles
	erys ears
557	nosethirles nostrils
558	bar carried
559	forneys furnace
560	janglere ... goliardeys gossip and a ribald talker
561	that his talk
561	harlotries dirty jokes
562	Wel koude ... thries he knew well how to steal corn and charge three times over
563	thombe of golde the proverb 'Every honest miller has a thumb of gold' means that there are no honest millers and few poor ones. The miller's thumb tested the corn and weighed out the flour
	pardee by God
565	sowne sound
566	therwithal he broughte with it he accompanied

LINES 567–86 THE MANCIPLE

A Manciple was a servant of a college or Inn of Court, who purchased the provisions under the direction of the cook and the steward. He is not a figure found in Estates satire.

CHECK THE BOOK

Jill Mann, *Chaucer and Medieval Estates Satire*, 1973, explains the tradition of social satire which supplied a platform for the Prologue.

Lines 567–86 The Maniciple continued

GLOSSARY

567	**gentil** pleasant
	temple the Middle and the Inner Temple are two of the lawyers' Inns of Court in London
568	**Of which achatours** from whom purchasers (caterers)
569	**vitaille** victuals
570	**taille** tally (notched on a tally-stick), credit
571	**algate** always
	wayted paid attention
	achaat buying
572	**ay biforn** always ahead
	staat state, condition
573	**grace** grace, favour
574	**lewed** uneducated (*not* lewd)
	wit intelligence
	pace surpass
575	**heep** heap
576	**maistres** masters, lawyers who have qualified by being called to the bar
576	**mo than thries** more than thrice
577	**of** in
	curious intimately interested
578	**duszeyne** dozen
579	**stywardes** stewards
581	**hym** the lord
	lyve by sustain himself upon
	propre good own property
582	**dettelees** without indebtedness
	but … wood unless he were mad
583	**scarsly** economically
	hym list desire it might please him to desire
584	**al a shire** a whole county
585	**caas** situation
	falle come about
586	**sette … cappe** set the caps of them all (made them look silly)

LINES 587–622 THE REEVE

A Reeve was the bailiff or factor for an estate: an estate-manager.
Like the Manciple, he makes dishonest profits. A trained carpenter,
he is later angered by the Miller's tale against a carpenter. The
Miller rides first, the Reeve last.

The Miller, the Manciple and the Reeve form a trio of dishonest
stewards. Compare them as frauds and as personalities (see
Characterisation, Stewards).

GLOSSARY

587	**sclendre colerik** thin, angry (see note on line 333)
588	**ny** nigh, near, close
589	**His heer ... yshorn** his hair was cut round his head at the height of his ears
590	**top was dokked** top was cut short. Priests wore a tonsure, but also kept their hair short
	biforn in front
591	**lene** lean
592	**Ylyk** like
	staf staff, stick
	ysene to be seen
593	**Wel ... bynne** he know how to take care of a granary and a corn-bin
594	**auditour** auditor, accountant
	on him wynne get the better of him
595	**wiste** knew
	droghte ... reyn drought and rain
596	**yeldynge** yield
597	**neet** cattle
598	**swyn his hors** swine (plural) and horses
	stoor livestock
	pultrye poultry
599	**governynge** control
600	**by his covenant** according to his agreement (legal deed of service)
	yaf the rekenynge gave the reckoning

**CHECK
THE BOOK**

Kolve, V.A., *Chaucer
and the Imagery of
Narrative*, 1984,
presents a profusely
illustrated account
of the pictorial
traditions
surrounding the
first five *Tales*.

Lines 587–622 The Reeve continued

CHECK THE BOOK

G.K. Chesterton's *Chaucer*, 1932, is the last pre-academic celebration of the poet, and still a marvellous book.

GLOSSARY	
601	Syn that since
602	brynge ... arrerage cause him to be behind (in collecting money due to him)
603	baillif bailiff, steward
	hierde shepherd
	hyne hind, servant
604	That ... covyne whose trickery and treachery he [the Reeve] did not know
605	adrad in dread, terrified
606	wonyng dwelling
608	purchace buy (land) (see notes on lines 320 and 575)
609	astored pryvely provisioned secretly
611	To yeve ... good to give and lend him from out of [the lord's] own goods
612	cote and hood the coat and hood were a servant's perquisite. Thanks are due to an equal or superior
613	myster trade, occupation (French *métier*). The Reeve is made a carpenter in order to lend point to the Miller's tale against a carpenter
615	stot horse, cob
616	pomely dapple
	highte was called
617	surcote of pers blue overcoat
619	Northfolk Norfolk, a county in East Anglia
620	toun village
	clepen Baldeswelle call Bawdswell
621	Tukked tucked. His robe was hitched up round him into his girdle, as a friar's is
	hyndreste of oure route hindmost of our crowd

LINES 623–68 THE SUMMONER

A Summoner summonsed accused persons to the Bishop's Court.

The Bishop's Court was presided over by an Archdeacon, who could impose fines backed by the threat of excommunication, which could lead to imprisonment by the civil authorities. So a summoner could easily extort money from the weak.

The Summoner is personally vicious, and also corrupt in the conduct of his office; the latter is regarded with more disfavour than the former. How should we read lines 655–62? (see **Characterisation, Ecclesiastical Villains**).

GLOSSARY

624	**fyr-reed … face** the face of a cherub, as red as fire. Although the faces of cherubs are traditionally red, the Summoner is not an angelic messenger
625	**saucefleem** pimpled (from 'salt phlegm')
	eyen narwe narrow eyes
626	**sparwe** sparrow; traditionally a lecher
627	**scalled** scaly, scabby
	piled scanty
629	**lytarge** white lead
630	**Boras** borax
	ceruce white lead
	tartre tartar
	noon not any kind
631	**byte** bite, scour
632	**whelkes** pimples
633	**knobbes** lumps
636	**crie** shout
	wood mad
640	**decree** decree (of canon law)
643	**Watte** Wat (short for 'Walter')
644	**grope** examine minutely, probe
646	**Ay … crie** he would always call out: 'Questio quid juris'. (Latin) 'I ask which law applies to this case'
647	**gentil harlot** easy-going rascal. ('Harlot' was applied exclusively to women only in the next century)
649	**suffer** allow
	for in return for
650	**have** keep, enjoy
	his the fellow's (not the Summoner's)
651	**atte fulle** at the end (of the year)
652	**a fynch … pulle** pluck the feathers of a finch (seduce a girl)

CONTEXT

Ecclesiastical law operated alongside civil law, and until the nineteenth century Church courts had jurisdiction over laity as well as clergy. Offences dealt with by these courts included sexual immorality, witchcraft and withholding of tithes.

CHECK THE BOOK

D.W. Robertson, Jr., *A Preface to Chaucer Criticism*, 1962, makes a formidably learned case for reading Chaucer against medieval traditions of spiritual allegory.

GLOSSARY

653   owher anywhere

a good felawe a good companion

655   ercedekenes curs archdeacon's curse, excommunication

656   But if unless

657   in his purs i.e., by a fine

658   helle an excommunicated person might go to hell for ever. The Summoner thinks a fine a worse punishment

659   woot ... dede know that in reality he was lying

660   Of cursyng ... drede every guilty man ought to be afraid of excommunication

For curs ... savith for excommunication will kill, just as absolution will save

662   And ... *Significavit* and he [the guilty man] should also beware of a *Significavit*. (The opening Latin word of a writ, issued by the Archdeacon to the civil authorities, certifying that an excommunicated man had remained obstinate after forty days; the penalty was imprisonment)

663   daunger jurisdiction, control

at ... gise to do with as he liked

664   girles the young of both sexes

diocise diocese (the area over which a bishop has responsibility)

665   hir conseil their secrets

al hir reed their only counsellor

666   gerland garland (of leaves and flowers)

667   greet large

ale-stake taverns used to advertise themselves by hanging a bush or garland from a pole outside

668   bokeleer buckler, shield

cake loaf (held in his lap)

LINES 669–714 THE PARDONER

A Pardoner sold pardons or indulgences. These were reductions or remissions of the punishment (penance) imposed upon the penitent in the confessional, or of punishment in Purgatory. (They are not the absolution from sin which a priest is empowered to give to a repentant sinner.)

The sale of indulgences was the abuse which occasioned the Reformation of the sixteenth century. The Pardoner is the last of the pilgrims, and the most corrupt.

Make sure you understand the distinction between pardon and absolution explained above. The portrait is full of false credentials as well as false relics.

What is the connection between the Pardoner's false pardons and his lack of masculinity?

Why is the Pardoner with the Summoner? (see **Characterisation, Ecclesiastical Villains**).

> **CONTEXT**
>
> Pardons were certificates of remission of penance, which had been introduced in return for gifts to an ecclesiastical charity (such as a hospital). The system of professional fund-raising got out of control and was abused, for example by unlicensed pardoners who sold false relics.

GLOSSARY

670	**Rouncivale** the hospital of St Mary, Rounceval, near Charing Cross, London. (Rounceval belonged to the Prior of Rouncevall in Navarre). The hotel above Charing Cross railway station was previously the hospital for which the Pardoner claims to be raising funds.
	compeer fellow, crony
671	**court of Rome** the Pardoner claims to come from the Roman Curia, the source of authorised indulgences
672	**'Com ... to me'** a popular song. The rhyme of 'Rome' and 'to me' confirms that -e was pronounced at the end of a line
673	**bar ... burdoun** accompanied him in a strong bass. (A homosexual relationship may be suggested)
674	**trompe** trumpet
675	**wex** wax
676	**But ... flex** but it hung straight, as does a hank of flax
677	**By ounces ... hadde** the few locks that he had hung separately
678	**And ... overspradde** and he spread them over his shoulders

Lines 669-714 The Pardoner continued

GLOSSARY

679	But ... oon but the hair lay in single strands
680	jolitee prettiness
681	walet pouch
682	Hym ... jet it seemed to him that he rode in the latest fashion
683	Dischevelee, save with hair unbound, except for
685	vernycle Veronica. (After St Veronica, who offered her veil to Christ on the way to Calvary so that he could wipe his face. The veil, with the impression of Christ's face, was kept at St Peter's in Rome. Pilgrims to Rome often wore copies of it)
686	lappe large pocket
687	Bretful full to the brim
	pardoun pardons
	hoot like cakes freshly made (part of the Pardoner's sales-talk)
688	smal ... goot thin as a goat has; that is, unbroken
690	late recently
691	trowe believe
	geldyng a castrated horse. The Pardoner is effeminate
692	fro ... Ware from Berwick-on-Tweed to Ware, Hertfordshire. (That is, in the whole length of England, as these towns are at each end of the Great North Road from Scotland to London)
694	male mail bag
	pilwe-beer pillowcase
695	Oure Lady veyl the veil of Our Lady (the Virgin Mary)
696	gobet gobbet, piece
	seyl sail
697	wente walked
698	see sea
	hente took up, saved (see Mark 15:7–11)
699	croys of latoun crucifix of brass
701	relikes relics. Until 1969, a Catholic altar had to incorporate a physical relic of a martyr. The cult of relics, a focus of popular piety, was often abused

CHECK THE BOOK

Peter Brown's *The Cult of the Saints*, 1982, illuminates the role played by relics – physical remains – in this cult. Without saints, there would have been no pilgrimages.

GLOSSARY

702	A povre ... lond a poor parson living in his country parish
703	Upon ... moneye in one day he got for himself more money
704	tweye two
705	feyned feigned
	japes tricks
706	apes gulls, fools
707	trewely to tellen to be serious
708	ecclesiaste the Pardoner was probably not a cleric
709	lessoun lesson (a Bible reading)
709	storie such as a Saint's Life, or the Pardoner's own moral tale
710	alderbest best of all
	offertorie anthem sung at the offertory (see line 450)
711	wiste knew
712	preche preach
	affile smooth
714	murierly more merrily

LINES 715–24 RECAPITULATION

GLOSSARY

715	clause short sentence
716	estaat condition
719	Belle the Bell, another hostelry
720	to yow ... telle to tell you
721	How ... nyght what we did with ourselves that same night
722	alyght alighted, settled
723	wol will
	viage journey

 CHECK THE BOOK
Steve Ellis in his *Geoffrey Chaucer*, 1996, a pamphlet in the British Council's Writers and their Work series, offers a lively introduction, keyed to the critical debates of the time of its publication.

LINES 725–46 APOLOGY

Chaucer apologises for gross language on the grounds that he is obliged to report the pilgrims' words exactly as they were spoken: a pretence which reminds us that the whole pilgrimage is a fiction. He then apologises for his recent negligence in not having put the pilgrims in order of rank. In fact he has observed precedence with some care: a joke which draws attention to the form of the fiction.

GLOSSARY

726	n'arette do not impute
	vileynye ill-breeding, grossness
728	cheere demeanour
729	Ne ... proprely not even if I speak their words, with accuracy in each case
730	al so as
732	He moot ... kan he should repeat, as closely, as he can
733	Everich every
	charge commission
734	Al ... large however rudely and freely he [the man of line 731] speak
735	untrewe falsely
736	feyne thyng feign things
737	spare relent
	he the man of line 731
738	moot as wel must impartially
739	Crist ... writ Christ himself spoke very broadly in the Scriptures
740	woot know
741	Eek ... rede also Plato says, whoever can read him. Almost no-one in England could read Greek, but this idea from the philosopher's *Timaeus* is mentioned in books Chaucer had translated
742	moote be cosyn must be cousin
744	Al if
	degree social rank
746	My wit is short I am not sufficiently clever

CONTEXT

Scholars have found historical originals for the pilgrims, but only the Host and Chaucer are certain. Chaucer fictionalises himself and perhaps the Host too.

THE TALE-TELLING GAME (LINES 747–858)

LINES 747–809 THE HOSTS PROPOSAL

The Host is as important to the *Tales* as any pilgrim, since he referees the tale-telling game. Later, the Cook calls him Harry Bailly; an innkeeper of this name is mentioned in the records for Southwark at this period.

Does his speech give a clue to his character? (see **The Road to Canterbury**).

❓ QUESTION
Why does the Host impose a tale-telling game?

GLOSSARY

747	**Greet … everichon** our host entertained us all very well
748	**soper** supper (a communal meal)
750	**leste** it pleased
751	**semely** suitable
	hooste Host, innkeeper
	withalle moreover, too
752	**For … halle** [fit] to have been a marshal [master of ceremonies] in a hall
753	**stepe** prominent
754	**Chepe** Cheapside, the market of the City of London. As Southwark was less respectable than the City, this is a compliment to the Host
755	**ytaught** instructed [in his trade]
756	**And … naught** he was in no way lacking in manhood
758	**pleyen** to play, jest
760	**maad our rekenynges** paid our bills
761	**lordynges** my masters [used like 'Ladies and Gentlemen']
762	**Ye … hertely** you are indeed heartily welcome to my house
764	**saugh nat** have not seen
765	**Atones** at one time
	herberwe harbour, inn
766	**Fayn … how** I would dearly like to entertain you, if I knew how

Lines 747–809 The Hosts Proposal continued

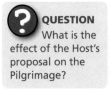

QUESTION
What is the effect of the Host's proposal on the Pilgrimage?

GLOSSARY	
767	bythoght struck by a thought
769	God yow speede may God bring you success
770	The blisful ... meede! May the blessed martyr [St Thomas] bring you your reward
771	wel I woot as I well know
	by the weye along the road
772	Ye ... pleye You intend to tell stories and amuse yourselves
773	is noon there is no
775	maken yow disport devise entertainment for you
776	erst first
777	yow liketh it pleases you
778	stonden at stand by, accept
779	werken do
781	Now ... deed Now by the soul of my father, who is dead
782	But ... heed! if you do not enjoy it, you can strike off my head
783	Hoold ... hondes in sign of agreement
784	Oure ... seche it did not take long to discover our opinion
785	Us ... wys we did not think it was worth while to deliberate seriously
786	avys consideration
787	voirdit ... leste whatever decision he pleased
788	quod said
	herkneth ... beste listen carefully
789	But ... desdeyn but do not treat it with disdain, I beg you
791	to ... weye so to shorten our journey
792	tweye two
793	To ... so I mean, on the way to Canterbury
794	And ... two and he shall tell another two on the way home
795	Of ... bifalle of adventures that have happened in the past
796	which the one
796	bereth hym manages
797	in this caas on this occasion
798	sentence meaning, significance
	solaas solace, comfort
799	oure aller cost the expense of the rest of us
801	agayn back

> **GLOSSARY**
>
> | | |
> |---|---|
> | 804 | Right ... cost at my own expense |
> | | gyde guide |
> | 805 | And ... withseye whoever shall dispute my judgement |
> | 806 | paye al pay for all |
> | 807 | vouche sauf grant |
> | 808 | anon ... mo immediately, without further discussion |
> | 809 | erly ... therefore get ready for the journey early |

 QUESTION Compare the pictures of the pilgrimage painted and engraved by Thomas Stothard and William Blake (see **Check the Net** on p.103).

LINES 810–21 THE TALE-TELLING GAME: THE PILGRIMS' ACCEPTANCE

Why do the pilgrims accept? What effect does it have on the pilgrimage (see **The Road to Canterbury**)?

> **GLOSSARY**
>
> | | |
> |---|---|
> | 810 | and ... swore and our oaths were sworn |
> | 813 | governour president |
> | 814 | juge and reportour judge and reporter |
> | 815 | And ... pris and arrange a supper at a set price |
> | 816 | reuled been be ruled |
> | | at his devys at his pleasure |
> | 817 | In ... assent in great things and small; and so, unanimously |
> | 819 | fet anon fetched immediately |
> | 820 | echon each of us |

LINES 822–58 THE TALE-TELLING GAME: THE SETTING-FORTH AND THE CUT

What is the implication of lines 835–41? What is the effect of line 844 (see **The Road to Canterbury**)?

> **GLOSSARY**
>
> | | |
> |---|---|
> | 822 | Amorwe in the morning |
> | 823 | cok cock, the male bird who leads the hens out |

Lines 822–58 The setting-forth and the cut continued

CONTEXT

The Knight gets the short straw; some theologians condemned the drawing of lots as the submission of free will to luck and fate.

GLOSSARY

825	**riden ... paas** rode at little more than a walking pace
826	**Wateryng ... Thomas** a stream where pilgrims watered their horses near the second milestone on the Canterbury road
827	**bigan ... areste** pulled his horse up
828	**leste** please
829	**Ye ... recorde** you know your promise, and I remind you of it
830	**If ... accorde** if evening-song and morning-song agree. (If you have not changed your tune)
832	**As ... ale** as I hope never to drink anything but wine or ale
835	**draweth** take. A polite plural imperative addressed to the more gentle pilgrims
	cut lots (Different lengths, perhaps of straw, are to be drawn from the Host's hand to decide who tells the first tale. The Host doubtless arranges that the Knight should draw the short straw)
	ferrer twynne depart further (from the inn)
838	**accord** decision
840	**lat ... shamefastnesse** leave aside your modesty
841	**Ne ... man!** stop dreaming: put out your hand and take your straw, everyone
842	**wight** man
844	**Were ... cas** either by luck, or fate, or chance
845	**sothe** sooth, truth
	fil fell
847	**And ... resoun** and tell his tale he must, as was reasonable
848	**foreward** agreement
	composicioun agreement
849	**han herd** have heard
	what ... mo more needs to be said?
851	**As he that** as a man who
853	**Syn** since
854	**a** by
855	**herkneth** listen!
857	**cheere** manner

EXTENDED COMMENTARIES

TEXT 1 – LINES 1-18 (THE OPENING SENTENCE)

(A rough rule for the pronunciation of final *-e* is to pronounce it only when it is required by the rhyme or metre. It is not pronounced when the next word begins with a vowel. Pronounce *e* when *italicised.*)

> Whan that Aprill with his shoures soot*e*
> The droght*e* of March hath perc*ed* to the root*e*,
> And bathed every veyne in swich licour
> Of which vertu engendred is the flour;
> 5   Whan Zephirus eek with his sweet*e* breeth
> Inspir*ed* hath in every holt and heeth
> The tendr*e* cropp*es*, and the yong*e* sonn*e*
> Hath in the Ram his half cours yronn*e*,
> And smal*e* fowel*es* maken melody*e*,
> 10 That slepen al the nyght with open y*e*
> (So priketh hem nature in hir corages),
> Thanne longen folk*e* to goon on pilgrimages,
> And palmeres for to seken straung*e* strond*es*,
> To fern*e* halw*es*, kowthe in sondry lond*es*;
> 15 And specially from every shir*es* end*e*
> Of Eng*e*lond to Caunterbury they wend*e*,
> The hooly blisful martir for to sek*e*,
> That hem hath holpen whan that they were seek*e*.

The Prologue has a fresh and joyful beginning: the spring urges the natural world into growth, birds into song and human beings to go on pilgrimage. These signs of spring are conveyed in a sentence of four clauses. The clauses are concerned with time (*Whan* in lines 1 and 5, *Thanne* in line 12), and then with place: *And specially* in line 15. The clauses address in turn the meteorological, vegetable, animal and human. This rhetorical device is called a chronographia, a literary setting in time and place; Chaucer had read such elevated openings to many of the Cantos of Dante's *Divine Comedy*, and he is imitating them. This sentence is far more formal than the rest of the Prologue, not only in its length and complex structure and phrasing (*in swich licour / Of which vertu*

CHECK THE BOOK

The first line of T.S. Eliot's poem of 1922, *The Waste Land*, 'April is the cruellest month....', twists the first line of the *Prologue*.

engendred is …), but also in its initial vocabulary which is scientific, mythological and astronomical. The references are explained in the **Detailed commentaries**. The sentence opens slowly and grandly, becomes lively with the *tendre croppes, the yonge sonne* and the *smale foweles* that cannot sleep, and finally comes home to human beings, and to Chaucer's home county of Kent. It is Nature that makes people *long* to go on pilgrimages, a natural instinct directed to a supernatural end: gratitude for the saint's intercession in heaven for those who have been sick but are now whole and healthy.

TEXT 2 – LINES 118-62 (THE PRIORESS)

Ther was also a Nonne, a PRIORESS*E*,
That of hir smylyng was ful symple and coy;
120 Hire gretteste ooth was but by Sein*te* Loy;
And she was cleped madame Eglentyn*e*.
Ful weel she soong the servic*e* dyvyn*e*,
Entun*ed* in hir nose ful semel*y*;
And Frenssh she spak ful faire and fetisly,
125 After the scole of Stratford att*e* Bow*e*,
For Frenssh of Parys was to hire unknow*e*.
At met*e* wel ytaught was she with all*e*;
She leet no morsel from hir lipp*es* fall*e*,
Ne wette hir fyngres in hir sauc*e* dep*e*;
130 Wel koude she carie a morsel and wel kep*e*
That no drop*e* ne fille upon hire brest.
In curteisi*e* was set ful muchel hir lest.
Hir over-lipp*e* wyp*ed* she so clen*e*
That in hir copp*e* ther was no ferthyng sen*e*
135 Of grec*e*, whan she dronken hadde hir draught*e*.
Ful semel*y* after hir met*e* she raught*e*.
And sikerly she was of greet desport,
And ful plesaunt, and amyable of port,
And peyned hire to countrefet*e* cheer*e*
140 Of court, and to been estatlich of maner*e*,
And to ben holden digne of reverenc*e*.
But for to speken of hir*e* conscienc*e*,
She was so charitable and so pitous
She wolde wepe, if that she saugh a mous
145 Kaught in a trapp*e*, if it were deed or bledd*e*.

Of smale houndes hadde she that she fedde
With rosted flessh, or milk and wastel-breed.
But soore wepte she if oon of hem were deed,
Or if men smoot it with a yerde smerte;
150   And al was conscience and tendre herte.
Ful semyly hir wympul pynched was,
Hir nose tretys, hir eyen greye as glas,
Hir mouth ful smal, and therto softe and reed.
But sikerly she hadde a fair forheed;
155   It was almoost a spanne brood, I trowe;
For, hardily, she was nat undergrowe.
Ful fetys was hir cloke, as I was war.
Of smal coral aboute hire arm she bar
A peire of bedes, gauded al with grene,
160   And theron heng a brooch of gold ful sheene,
On which ther was first write a crowned A,
And after *Amor vincit omnia*. (lines 118–62)

CHECK THE BOOK
The Riverside Chaucer, the standard edition of his works (ed. L.D. Benson, 1987) has an excellent 100 page glossary, too often neglected by students.

This portrait is selected as a sample of Chaucer's art and of the problems of interpretation and tone set by his habit of praise. It is hard to assess the degree of criticism in the portrait, an assessment complicated by changes in the meaning of words and by modern unfamiliarity with the ideals and historical realities of the life of nuns. Such factors – ironical praise, changes in sense, and historical ignorance – play a part in interpreting almost all the portraits.

Deficiency of knowledge may be remedied more easily than prejudice. Religious orders were suppressed at the Protestant Reformation of the sixteenth century, and many people of today, even among Christians, may have little understanding or experience of the ideal of the celibate single life dedicated to Christ. Since Prioresses often came from aristocratic families or gentry, ladylike bearing and courtly table manners are no surprise. Most *gentil* families had members in religious orders; Chaucer has a sister or a daughter who was a nun. Madame Eglentyne's name, nose, eyes, mouth and forehead are well bred. Little dogs and gold brooches were not in the Benedictine Rule; yet the Rule had been modified over the centuries; the Prioress's little weaknesses do not in themselves indicate personal laxity. Key words which have changed sense are *coy*, which means 'quiet' not 'archly inviting'; *countrefete*

CHECK THE BOOK

In his *Social Chaucer*, 1989, Paul Strohm argues that the *Prologue* and the *Tales* offer a reconciliation of competing elements in society.

means 'imitate' not 'fake'. These considerations make the portrait less broadly satiric and more ironic.

But ambiguity is systematic. We have to recognise the ambiguities rather than hope to resolve them all. The motto on the brooch could be either religious or secular (see **Detailed commentaries**). We are to smile at the nun's French accent, too-perfect manner and pity for very small animals, but whether her nasal singing, her height and her large forehead deserve a smile is not so clear (large foreheads, for example, were fashionably beautiful in the late fourteenth century). The question is complicated by the recurrent use in the portraits of hyperbole and the superlative. Chaucer's work often shows amusement at human vanity generally, not just feminine vanity. But how gentle is this satire, and how severe? Madame Eglentyne is certainly too concerned with manner, and seems to care more for mice than for men. The society lady's devotion to pets is an enduring comic stereotype. Older critical reaction is summed up in a phrase of the critic John Livingstone Lowes: 'the engagingly imperfect submergence of the feminine in the ecclesiastical'. Recent views of this portrait have been affected by outrage at the antisemitism of the Tale the Prioress later tells. But to see this nun and everything about her as ridiculous or worse would be a serious mistake. Chaucer is judgemental only in extreme cases. He does not here repudiate the celibate ideal, nor does he condemn the nun's softness. He carefully leaves plenty of room for interpretation. We too have to listen carefully – and we do not have to make up our minds.

TEXT 3 – LINES 331-60 (THE FRANKLIN)

A FRANKELEYN was in his compaigny*e*.
Whit was his berd as is the dayesy*e*;
Of his complexioun he was sangwyn.
Wel loved he by the morwe a sop in wyn;
335 To lyven in delit was evere his won*e*,
For he was Epicurus owene son*e*,
That heeld opinioun that pleyn delit
Was verray felicitee parfit.
An housholder*e*, and that a greet, was he;
340 Seint Julian he was in his contree.
His breed, his al*e*, was alweys after oon;

> A bettre envyn*ed* man was nowher noon.
> Withoute bak*e* met*e* was nevere his hous,
> Of fissh and flessh, and that so plentevous
> 345   It snewed in his hous of mete and drynk*e*;
> Of alle deyntees that men koud*e* thynk*e*,
> After the sondry sesons of the yeer,
> So chaung*ed* he his mete and his soper.
> Ful many a fat partrich hadde he in muw*e*,
> 350   And many a breem and many a luce in stuw*e*.
> Wo was his cook but if his sauc*e* wer*e*
> Poynaunt and sharp, and redy al his geer*e*.
> His tabl*e* dormant in his hall*e* alway
> Stood redy covered al the long*e* day.
> 355   At sessiouns ther was he lord and sir*e*;
> Ful oft*e* tyme he was knyght of the shir*e*.
> An anlaas and a gipser al of silk
> Heeng at his girdel, whit as morn*e* milk.
> A shirreve hadd*e* he been, and a contour.
> 360   Was nowher swich a worthy vavasour. (lines 331–60)

It is a good exercise to try to make a literal translation of selected passages of this short text. Here is an attempt to do so for this portrait:

In his company was a Franklin. His beard was as white as a daisy; he was sanguine of complexion. In the morning he dearly loved a cake dipped in wine. Always to live in pleasure was his settled habit, for he was a true son of Epicurus, who held the view that true and perfect happiness consisted in pleasure itself. He was a householder, and a great one: in his part of the world he was St Julian. His bread and his ale were always of the same quality; and nowhere was there a man with a better cellar. His house was never without baked dishes of fish and flesh, and they were in such plenty that in his house it snowed meat and drink, and all conceivable delicacies. He changed his diet and his table according to the various seasons of the year. He had a great many fat partridges in coops, and many a bream and many a pike in ponds. It was a bad day for his cook if his sauce was not piquant and sharp, or if his equipment was not ready. There was always a table, covered and set, standing in his hall all day long. At the Quarter

> **? QUESTION**
> Does the amount of physical detail in a portrait such as the Franklin's suggest that Chaucer was a materialist?

Text 3 lines 331–60 (The Franklin) continued

Sessions he was lord and master and sat many times as Knight of the Shire. A dagger, and a purse made all of white silk as white as morning milk hung from his belt. He had been a sheriff and an auditor. Nowhere was there such a splendid landholder.

This landholder does not live off the community, as many of the professionals do. He is as hospitable as St Julian, the patron saint of hospitality: his table stands there for all who come. But he is also an epicure: his delicious food is for himself (although it is the philosopher Epicurus, not the Franklin, who is said here to be dedicated to pleasure – *delit*.) The old man shows the same gusto in life that makes even the most wayward pilgrim so enjoyable. The Franklin's way of life is picturesquely described, with poetic figures (lines 332, 345–6, 358); the final lines list the public offices that had brought the Sergeant into contact with him.

The picture of country hospitality, the first of many in English, is done with a Chaucerian combination of cordiality, freshness, slight hyperbole ('It *snewed* in his hous of mete and drynke') and affectionate mockery, as in:

> Ful many a fat partrich hadde he in muwe,
> And many a breem and many a luce in stuwe. (lines 349–50)

It is at the rhyme that the wit becomes apparent:

CONTEXT

Rime riche, the rhyming of identical words, e.g. 'wyn/sangwyn', was appreciated, not avoided.

> Whit was his berd as is a dayseye.
> Of his complexioun he was sangwyn.
> Wel loved he by the morwe a sop in wyn. (lines 332–4)

The simple, factual lines succeed each other without criticism, yet the rhyming of *sangwyn* with *wyn* suggests that the wine may have helped the blood in producing the Franklin's ruddy complexion. (Such identical rhyme was admired.) The good living of the Franklin, even his testiness towards his cook, is regarded indulgently, if one can go by the innocence of the comparisons to the daisy and morning milk. The Franklin is both attractive and a caricature; such an engaging combination shows Chaucer's grasp and his humanity.

PART THREE

CRITICAL APPROACHES

LITERARY GENRES AND MODES

The General Prologue draws on several different genres or kinds of writing. It is a prologue (preface, foreword) in which the author speaks to his audience, introducing a larger work. A medieval prologue aimed to capture the good will of its auditors and readers, to lay out what is to follow, and to apologise for any inadequacies. This prologue consists of a formal opening (lines 1–18); the introduction of the pilgrimage and of the narrator (lines 19–41); a catalogue of portraits of his companions (lines 42–714); the apology (lines 725–46); the setting-up of the tale-telling game (lines 747–821); the riding out, and the drawing of lots for who shall tell the first tale (lines 822–58).

The catalogue of portraits takes up almost four-fifths of the Prologue. Detailed description can become static, and catalogues can become repetitious. But Chaucer varies his approach and is unpredictable. His prologue is also a narrative: each pilgrim is described not only in terms of his or her profession, appearance and character but also in terms of how they strike their fellow-pilgrim, Chaucer. He half dramatises many of them, conveying the impression that they have spoken to him and that he is passing on what they say. This relationship between the narrator and his creations keeps the descriptions alive. The narrative quickens in the final section as the Host chivvies and persuades the pilgrims, leads them out of Southwark, and arranges the cut so that the Knight should tell the first tale.

As well as prologue, description and narrative, the General Prologue also draws on the materials of **satire**. Satire is the holding up to ridicule of folly and vice, and medieval satire attacked its victims harshly. Satire of the three estates of medieval society caricatured the typical faults of the members of the military, clerical and lay estates, as in *Piers Plowman*, which has a hunting monk, a flattering friar and some venal laymen, types who also appear in Chaucer. But Chaucer uses a different approach, partly drawn from

CHECK THE BOOK

John Burrow is a leading British critic of medieval literature. His *Medieval Writers and their Work: Middle English Literature and its Background 1100-1500*, of 1982, is a fine general introduction.

CHECK THE BOOK

John Burrow's *Ricardian Poetry: Gower, Langland and the 'Gawain' poet*, 1971, put forward an influential view of the poetry written in Richard II's troubled reign.

the thirteenth-century French *Roman de la Rose,* an encyclopaedic narrative work, the beginning of which he had translated as *The Romaunt of the Rose.* The French poem is a **dream-vision,** in which a dreamer meets and describes various personages, who talk and interact with him. The *Roman* does not attack the targets of its satire but allows them to speak. Chaucer does likewise, and he develops a technique of **ironical praise,** examined below. Thus the Prologue uses a number of genres, modes and approaches. It is not a work of naïve realism or of straightforward social observation, although it contains elements which have allowed modern readers accustomed to realism to read much of it in that way.

Something must now be said of the work which the Prologue introduces. *The Canterbury Tales* is a very varied miscellany of tales such as might conceivably be told by a mixed group of pilgrims on the road to Canterbury, though really a collection of stories written or re-written by Chaucer. The work is united by the framework of the tale-telling competition, and though the pilgrims do not even reach Canterbury, a pattern is clear. At its simplest it is a compilation of various stories set inside two frame-stories, the pilgrimage and the Hosts's tale-telling game. The Prologue sets up the game, and it also sets up the human players at the beginning of its own game. The Host's game nearly comes to a halt as soon as the Knight finishes the first tale. The Host's authority is flouted by the drunken Miller, who insults him and the Knight and the Reeve. Pilgrims quarrel and fall out of charity. The Knight later stops the Host attacking the Pardoner. Chaucer's tale is stopped by the Host. Some pilgrims do not speak, others talk a lot, notably the Wife of Bath. Tales are interrupted or stopped by the Host or other pilgrims. A runaway servant rides up and joins the pilgrimage. Finally the drunken Cook falls off his horse, and the Parson tells the last tale. The frame-story is social comedy, not without a hint of the more serious purpose of a pilgrimage. Some tales are very serious indeed. The *Canterbury Tales* is far from being the crude romp it usually becomes in modern adaptations for stage and screen.

Only two of the early manuscripts contain all the tales. In other manuscripts the Tales survive in ten groupings, or manuscript 'fragments', as follows:

Fragment   I: General Prologue, Tales of the the Knight, Miller and Cook

       II: Man of Law's Tale

     III: Tales of the Wife of Bath, Friar and Summoner

     IV: Tales of the Clerk and Merchant

     V: Tales of the Squire and Franklin

    VI: Tales of the Physician and Pardoner

   VII: Tales of the Shipman, Prioress, Chaucer (two, Sir Thopas, and Melibee), the Monk, and the Nuns' Priest

  VIII: Tales of the Second Nun and the Canon's Yeoman (a runaway servant who joins the pilgrims)

    IX: Manciple's Tale

    X: Parson's Tale, Chaucer's Retraction.

Most of these Tales have prologues and/or epilogues, sometimes interrupted the Host or by other pilgrims.

The Canterbury Tales is a large miscellany. In the standard edition, the Riverside Chaucer, the text takes up well over three hundred double-column pages of print in rather small type.

The General Prologue is an expository introduction and overture to the *Tales*, hinting at some of the themes as well as introducing the tellers of the tales. Because it is varied and self-contained, and as vividly detailed as medieval manuscript illuminations, it is often read on its own. Thus detached, it becomes a picture of the society of the time, especially as the gallery of portraits of the pilgrims is a cross-section of those who were free to go on a pilgrimage. It is also written in a lively and realistic style, so that we can imagine that Chaucer did meet actual people resembling his fellow-pilgrims. Chaucer's story-telling art allows us to combine with the interest of understanding something of medieval society the pleasure of becoming involved with a 'real' set of people.

The Prologue was, however, intended as a prologue, something 'spoken before'. Chaucer probably read it aloud to friends and at court, and wrote it so that we should imagine him doing so. Audiences who knew Chaucer would have enjoyed the idea of his

CHECK THE BOOK

Even if you use a smaller edition of the Prologue, you should take a good look at the Riverside Chaucer to get an idea of the *Tales* as a whole.

accidentally falling in with a ready-made group of pilgrims and of their fictional adventures. They would have certainly been amused at the figure Chaucer cuts later on in the *Tales*. The Host addresses him as a fat little man, too shy to tell a story. When pressed, the pilgrim Chaucer begins on a feeble romance, a **parody** of bad popular romances: it rhymes so wretchedly that the Host cannot endure it and rudely prevents his own author from continuing. Like the original audience, we know that this supposedly autobiographical story is not true. Chaucer may have gone on such a pilgrimage, but it is not likely that its members spoke in verse, nor that their tales would have been audible from horseback. The appearance of **verisimilitude** is brilliant and at times intense, but it is a deliberate illusion. Chaucer often dispenses with this verisimilitude: many of the tales are fantastic, whether adventurous, miraculous, indecent or farcical. Some tales are doctrinal; the Parson's is not a story but a treatise on penance. The second tale Chaucer himself tells, the Tale of Melibeus and Prudence, is a sober moral allegory recommending patience. The verisimilitude of the Prologue is only one of his literary modes.

CHECK THE BOOK

The journal *Chaucer Review* carries articles and reviews, and updates the bibliography of Chaucer studies.

Chaucer has an eye for social realities, but it would not have occurred to him to write social history or a naturalistic novel. The pilgrims were dreamed up in order that the tales which are to follow should have tellers to tell them. On examination, each of the portraits proves to be formal and self-contained, as they are not in novels. Also each pilgrim belongs to a different profession, except for the Second Nun and five Guildsmen. This suggests that Chaucer meant to show a representative cross-section of society, as in estates satire, in which the faults of the three estates were held up for correction. He includes only those who were likely to go on such a pilgrimage. Pilgrimages would not include serfs or poor peasants not free to travel. A nobleman would travel with his own retinue. Thus the base and apex of the feudal pyramid are not here. There are twenty-six men and three women: women would normally stay at home unless, like the Prioress and her opposite number the Wife of Bath, they were independent.

Chaucer could not guess that readers six centuries later would think of him and his pilgrims as typically medieval. His purposes differed from those of, for example, George Eliot, who certainly meant the characters of her novel *Middlemarch* (published in 1872) to represent the historical life of a Midlands town in the early nineteenth century. So long as we bear this difference in mind, there is no harm in seeing the pilgrims as English men and women of the later Middle Ages. They are presented as typical human beings, and have social and economic as well as moral and spiritual dimensions. Many of them are types who would have been familiar to lettered and unlettered people in the audience: the hunting monk, the venal friar, the dedicated knight, the gay young squire, the ladylike prioress, the good parson. All these were figures known to popular as well as literary tradition, as caricatures or as ideals. The central figure of the slightly earlier poem *Piers Plowman* is an idealised ploughman, like Chaucer's ploughman.

QUESTION When do the Middle Ages begin and end? What is the thinking behind this periodisation?

The portraits belong in the Prologue as part of a developing fictional action. To use a theatrical analogy, it is as if *The Canterbury Tales* were a play which opened with the cast assembled on the stage at the beginning instead of at the end. A true historical sense involves us in seeing these characters as living: when we see the Merchant, we see a pompous businessman, not just a typical representative of an emerging class in the City of London in the late fourteenth century. Later on he turns out to be unhappily married, and becomes a typical human being as well as a typical merchant.

CHAUCER AND NARRATIVE

The Prologue is highly unusual in that its narrator is also a character in his own fiction. The author acts as reporter. After the initial description of spring, we hear (lines 30–2) how Chaucer made himself one of the pilgrims:

> And shortly, whan the sonne was to reste,
> So hadde I spoken with hem everichon
> That I was of hir felaweshipe anon … (lines 30–2)

We gather that Chaucer was a sociable pilgrim; his previous comments on the accommodation at the Tabard indicate that he appreciated its amenity and enjoyed company. (People travelled the roads in companies for security reasons; some of the pilgrims are armed. We know that Chaucer was robbed two or three times.) Chaucer tells us that he had a 'ful devout corage' (line 22), but medieval religion did not stop him enjoying convivial company. Days spent on pilgrimage were both holy days and holidays. The modesty with which he offers to describe his companions confirms him as affable and unaffected.

But we know quite a lot about the public life and career of this disarming fellow, and his audience knew more, for he had written many poems in which he presents himself in a similar way. He was an experienced king's man, a diplomat, an MP, a JP, a retired customs officer. It was his job to win people's confidence, to get them talking. He knew his fellow men and the tricks they get up to. The original audience knew things about Chaucer that we cannot know – especially if they had seen and heard him read his works. But thanks to scholars and to a reading of his earlier works, we can be sure that his previous reputation played a part in the reception of the tale he is now beginning.

? QUESTION
When does the phase of the English language called Middle English begin and end? Where does this periodisation come from?

He says in lines 35–42 that he thinks it reasonable, before he goes any further in his literary adventure, to tell us the condition, occupation, rank and dress of each of his companions. The military estate is described without any obvious **irony**. But we do not have to read very far into the description of the Prioress (lines 118–62) to realise that, however uncomplicated and impressionable Chaucer the pilgrim may pretend to be, he conveys things about the other pilgrims that seem to be beyond the easy-going fellow who made himself a member of their company. Chaucer the pilgrim seems to be very impressed by the Prioress's ladylike manners, yet makes us aware that her charity is directed toward her dogs. Love, for the Prioress, conquers all (line 162), and Chaucer too seems to be under the influence. At the outset of the portrait of the Monk, our suspicions are further aroused. We are told that the Monk was 'a manly man, to been an abbot able'. The idea that manliness qualifies a monk to be an abbot is comic, since monks are vowed to celibacy. This sounds like a standard contemporary joke against monks. But could it also be a joke at the expense of the simplicity of the speaker, the pilgrim named Chaucer? Or at anyone who entertains the notion that the qualification for becoming abbot is a commandingly masculine appearance? Immediately afterwards we hear that the bells on the Monk's bridle rang 'als cleere / And eek as loude as dooth the chapel belle' (line 171). We already know that the Monk (who is vowed to poverty) has many horses and is fond of hunting (monastic estates offered plenty of land to hunt over). This last line insinuates, once again in a slyly comic way, that the Monk obeyed the summons of the hunt more promptly than that of the chapel. Is the pilgrim narrator unconscious of this irony, and the straightfaced poet enjoying a little joke? This variable perspective haunts the Prologue.

The pleasant sociability of the pilgrim Chaucer may well have been part of his creator's own character: social ease is part of the diplomat's life. Chaucer's disciple, the fifteenth-century poet John Lydgate, testified that Chaucer 'seyde alwey the beste'. Yet retired customs officers, however agreeable, are not impressionable. We sense a play between the narrator and the poet. Is the man in the poem the same as the man who wrote the poem and read it to his audiences? This question was first put and answered (negatively) by E.T. Donaldson in his *Speaking of Chaucer*, 1970, but it has been sensed by all who have enjoyed what the American poet Ezra Pound called 'the Chaucerian chuckle'. It follows that we do not always accept what the speaker says about the other pilgrims, nearly all of whom seem to impress him hugely, with the exception of the low-class rogues who bring up the rear. The gallery of portraits is thus viewed from two angles simultaneously – the social surface of every character, as disclosed to the narrator's innocent eye, but with something of each pilgrim's inner nature also, disclosed by the poet.

 CHECK THE BOOK
In his elegant *Speaking of Chaucer*, 1970, E.T. Donaldson formulated a (still popular) distinction between Chaucer the impressionable pilgrim, and his creator.

Another way of taking this is not to separate Chaucer-the-pilgrim from Chaucer-the-poet, but to regard it all as part of his irony. Irony is a rhetorical technique, critical discussions of which can become very complicated. But it is a speech-habit common in everyday life. Essentially, it means saying one thing while conveying another. Thus, some of the many pilgrims Chaucer calls 'worthy' seem entirely unworthy (the Friar, for example). Among those whom he calls good fellows are the Shipman, a thief, and the Summoner, a corrupt officer of the church court. A more complex instance of irony is when Chaucer tells us in line 183 that he *said* that the Monk's opinion was good. The Monk has just given it as his opinion that holy men may hunt, and that a monk need not stay in his cloister. But Benedictine monks take a vow of stability: to stay in the monastery to praise God in the liturgy and the monastic office of prayer, rather than rolling about the world. The Rule of St Benedict also enjoins study and manual labour, and the renunciation of the world and of personal possessions – such as a stable of fine horses. It is clear that the Monk does not observe the Benedictine Rule, and strains even a relaxed observance of that Rule. It is clear too that the reader is to notice this contradiction. To the original audience, the hunting Monk was a familiar figure of **satire**: a well-mounted gentleman in a well-filled habit, who once strayed into the cloister and has now strayed out of it: a rubicund renouncer of this world, riding in the medieval equivalent of a Rolls-Royce and enjoying it.

**CHECK
THE BOOK**
The *Chaucer
Yearbook*, an
annual publication,
is a place in which
to catch up on
recent scholarship.

But Chaucer does not denounce the Monk. On the contrary, he praises him, agrees with him, admires his splendid horse, boots, physique, taste and diet. Irony relies for its success on the knowledge and alertness of the audience. This is more reliable when the author reads his poem facing his audience than when his written text is read silently by readers remote in time or place. Some critics think that the play of Chaucer's irony, habitual even in his early writings, is not well served by drawing a hard and fast distinction between the pilgrim Chaucer and the poet Chaucer. They prefer that we should imagine ourselves in the original audiences who listened to Chaucer, knowing him and knowing that he was by no means the impressionable person or **persona** he presents in the Prologue. They prefer to describe the effect of these disparities between what is said and what is meant as irony. We certainly should compare Chaucer's expressed opinions with what he tells us elsewhere in a portrait. Whether we talk about pilgrim and poet, or whether we talk about irony, makes little difference. But it is essential not to take everything Chaucer says simply at face value.

It should be recognised that a naïve or gullible narrator is common in fiction – as in Swift's *Gulliver's Travels* (1726). It was especially common in the **dream-vision** poems so prominent in the narrative literature of the thirteenth and fourteenth centuries. Two of the poems Chaucer imitated, the French *Romance of the Rose* and Dante's *Divine Comedy*, were dream-visions in which the dreamer is ignorant and has to be instructed by the figures he meets in his dream, and particularly by his guide. Three of the greatest English poems of Chaucer's day were dream-visions also: Langland's *Piers Plowman*, Gower's *Confessio Amantis* and the anonymous *Pearl*. Chaucer translated the first part the *Roman de la Rose*. Except for *Troilus and Criseyde* all his longer poems before the *Tales* are dream-visions. Chaucer often makes himself a comic figure in these early poems, and is always having a joke with the audience in a way often thought to be characteristically English. There was, then, nothing surprising in the idea of Chaucer asking us to laugh at him as well as with him. In the language of the comic stage, Chaucer the pilgrim is the 'straight man' who allows the people he meets to do all the talking – and to give themselves away in the process.

A frequent feature of the dream-vision was that the dreamer met at the outset a number of personified abstractions whose portraits are given in series. That is how the *Romance of the Rose* begins, and J.V. Cunningham pointed out that the General Prologue adapts this useful expository device into a more realistic mode. Chaucer's adaptation has been so successful that the origins of this device of the dreamer in the portrait-gallery have been forgotten.

The final section of the Prologue, in which the pilgrims accept the Host's proposal of a tale-telling game, in which he is to be the judge, is also illuminated by this parallel with the dream-vision. The Host becomes the pilgrims' guide, and all the pilgrims agree to obey him. Like the guides in Chaucer's early poems, the Host is a manipulator – talkative, uncontrollable and slightly mischievous. As master of the game, he is not altogether a suitable figure to preside over a pilgrimage: he drinks and swears, and teases and bullies the less important pilgrims, notably Chaucer himself. Rather like Falstaff at the end of Shakespeare's *Henry IV*, he overdoes things, and has to be snubbed at the end; in this case by the Parson. A richly comic character, the Host plays many roles in the pilgrimage.

Contemporary audiences, however, would have noticed that the innocent narrator's confidence was easily won by the Host, and would also have been familiar with stories where a rash promise

CHECK THE BOOK

For an original yet scholarly view of the *Prologue*, see J.V. Cunningham. 'Convention as Structure – The Prologue to *The Canterbury Tales*' in *Geoffrey Chaucer: A Critical Anthology*, ed. J.A. Burrow (1969) pp. 218–32.

CONTEXT

'Merrie England':
the standard
formula in ballads
and popular
literature for pre-
Reformation
England. The
Reformers
suppressed the
celebration of
Christmas and
other popular
feasts.

(such as all the pilgrims make to obey the Host) turns out alarmingly. The Host of the Tabard is a jolly character, and has often been seen as the incarnation of a Merrie England unreformed by the puritan Reformation. He does indeed turn the pilgrimage into a merry game, a rather mad game, but by the same token we must expect such a figure to be dethroned at the end – as the Lord of Misrule was in medieval comic plays. Indeed the Pardoner, an expert on drinking, describes the tavern as the devil's temple. But he was sitting in a pub at the time, and is later exposed as a fake by the Host himself. It would be a grave mistake to see the Host as a figure of the Devil – after all, Chaucer's family had made their living by selling drink – but it would also be a mistake to take him, or any of the pilgrims, as Chaucer the pilgrim does, entirely at their face value.

Finally, to complete Chaucer's humorous presentation of himself, we should know of his later appearance in *The Canterbury Tales*. In the Prologue to Sire Thopas the Host calls upon Chaucer to tell a tale:

GLOSSARY

artow art thou

quod said

woldest wouldst

war yow pay attention

waast waist

> And seyde thus: 'What man artow?' quod he;
> 'Thou lookest as thou woldest fynde an hare,
> For evere upon the ground I se thee stare.
> Approche neer, and looke up murily.
> Now war yow, sires, and lat this man have place.
> He in the waast is shape as wel as I ...   (lines 695–700)

The Host, who is stout, is having a joke at Chaucer's girth:

> This were a popet in an arm t'enbrace
> For any womman, smal and fair of face.
> He semeth elvyssh by his contenaunce,
> For unto no wight dooth he daliaunce. (Lines 700–704)

GLOSSARY

popet doll

t'enbrace to embrace

smal slender

fair attractive

elvyssh elflike

contenaunce look

For ... daliaunce he
pays court to no man

Chaucer has hardly begun his tale of Sir Thopas when the Host stops him with extreme rudeness. Chaucer punishes this bumptious creature by telling another tale, about Melibee, a long moral allegory stuffed with wise sentences and maxims in which Prudence advises her hot-tempered husband Melibeus to be patient.

CHARACTERISATION

Chaucer's characterisation in the General Prologue is celebrated.
But before we look at the portraits, we should notice their order.
Beforehand, Chaucer says (lines 30–42) that he will tell us about the
state, profession, rank and appearance of each of the pilgrims, but
afterwards apologises for his informality: 'Also I prey yow to
foryeve it me, / Al have I nat set folk in hir degree' (lines 743–4).
This apology draws attention to the order, and turns out to be
partly a joke, for he has in fact set folk in their degree, according to
a hierarchy both social and moral: the good Knight at the top and
the fraudulent Pardoner at the bottom. It is true that the final
bunch of pilgrims, the rogues, seem to have been tagged on (line
541) almost as an afterthought. But in general Chaucer has
observed the rule of precedence which the social hierarchy dictated.
Feudal precedence was being challenged by the power of new
money, and by the numbers of men leaving the manor after the
Black Death to seek paid work in towns. Equality, except before
God, was not a principle of medieval social theory.

THE ESTATES

The military estate is followed by the clerical estate; the clerics by
the laity; an upper-middle class by a lower-middle class; with the
rascals at the end. Further, within this apparently casual order of
descending importance and merit, there is an order created by
contrasts in juxtaposition: the Knight fights for his lord, the Squire
for his lady; the Merchant talks of his prospering business, the
Clerk of moral virtue; the Clerk's cope is threadbare, the Friar's is
new. On inspection, the catalogue is found to have moral patterns.
It is not, as Chaucer pretends, a set of notes on some striking
individuals, nor a social cross-section of interest to historians.

The order of appearance goes like this (with the number of lines in
each portrait given in brackets):

(1) Military estate: Knight (35 lines), Squire (21), Yeoman (16): 72
                       in all

(2) Clerical estate: Prioress (44), Monk (43), Friar (61): 148

CONTEXT

In the Peasants'
Revolt of 1381 the
Archbishop of
Canterbury was
murdered, and the
palace of John of
Gaunt burnt down.

The Estates continued

(3) Professionals: Merchant (14), Clerk (23), Sergeant of the
                       Law (21), Franklin (29), Guildsmen (18),
                       Cook (8), Shipman (23), Doctor (33) and Wife
                       of Bath (32) : 201

(4) Good Men: Parson (51), Ploughman (12): 63

(5) Stewards: Miller (21), Manciple (19), Reeve (35): 75

(6) Church Officers: Summoner (45), Pardoner (45): 90

Medieval social theory divided the king's subjects into three estates:
the Military, the Clergy and the Laity. Chaucer observes this
division, although the Clerk and Parson, a member of the secular
clergy, are included with the Laity rather than with those in religous
orders. The Laity – groups 3, half of 4, and 5 – are arranged in only a
rough order of precedence, unlike the first two estates. The Sergeant
of the Law, for example, might outrank the two men introduced
before him, and the Franklin, as an established landholder, might
outrank the newly rich Sergeant. These minor departures from
precedence make the catalogue seem more impromptu, casual and
informal. The Laity are divided into three groups here: the
financially independent professionals, and those who work for them;
with, between the two, in pointed contrast the Parson and
Ploughman, men poor in the things of this world but free from
hypocrisy and avarice. Finally, we have the ecclesiastical villains.

The estate of the regular clergy gets twice as many lines as the
military one, reflecting the volume of anti-clerical **satire**. The
portraits of the Summoner and the Pardoner are also lengthy. As
for the third estate, it is noticeable that everyone in groups 3, 5 and
6 is on the make. The only clear exception is the Clerk, who stands
in stark contrast between the Merchant and the Sergeant. The
Military are exempt from the bourgeois vice of greed, and so are
the senior Clergy except for the Friar, though the Monk and the
Prioress are a very comfortable lord and lady who happen to be in
religious orders.

**CHECK
THE BOOK**

*Studies in the Age
of Chaucer* is an
annual publication
in which current
scholarship can be
accessed. Its scope
is not limited to just
Chaucer.

THE MILITARY

Knights had dominated English society since the Norman Conquest, and Chaucer begins his catalogue with a shining example of Christian chivalry, setting an ideal standard, of which nearly all the other pilgrims fall short.

THE KNIGHT

The Knight is defined in terms of his virtues (lines 45–6) and actions to defend the faith, far more than by his appearance and words. The Knight is also distinguished from his son, who has fought against fellow-Christians in France, whereas the Knight's motive is religious. In his courtesy to all and his modest dress he completes the figure of the off-duty soldier as Christian gentleman, and is one of three pilgrims who are presented as admirable. Like the Parson and the Ploughman, the worthy Knight is the ideal of his estate.

All the pilgrims are superlative: each is the perfect example of his or her type and/or profession. The Knight is the antique pattern of the chivalry of Edward III's time.

THE SQUIRE

The Squire is a type of gallant young lover, fresh and fashionable, perhaps like some in the court audience. His description is an example of the principle of contrast which governs much of the arrangement of the Prologue, even down to apparently casual detail. The Knight had good horses but was not gay in appearance himself (line 74); indeed his coarse tunic is all rusty. His son dresses like a picture of the spring; he cuts a fine figure on a horse (line 94), but no horse is mentioned. The father fights in his lord's war, and has thrice slain his foe; for his part, the son has done well for a beginner in his *chyvachie* across the Channel, in the hope of gaining his lady's favour. (Chaucer himself had been a French prisoner-of-war by the time he was twenty; the Black Prince, Edward III's son and Richard II's father, had led the English army into battle at the age of fifteen.) The Squire's prowess is that of a lover: like the birds of lines 9–11, he does not sleep at night. If he is treated with some

> **QUESTION**
> 'Although the gallery of portraits is static, the commentary which introduces them to us makes it seem dynamic.' Assess the truth of this.

amusement, the Squire is harmless; Chaucer's attitude seems indulgent rather than censorious, not unlike that of Duke Theseus in the Knight's Tale towards the young lovers Palamon and Arcite: Theseus remembers that he was a lover himself when young. And the Squire is a dutiful son.

THE YEOMAN

The Yeoman's portrait is vividly pictorial, but anonymous. In keeping with medieval admiration for professional skill, the adverb Chaucer chooses to describe the way the Yeoman looked after his *takel* is 'yeomanlike'. He is every inch an archer and a forester, resplendent in the badges of his trade. The archers in the English army were instrumental in winning the battles of the Hundred Years War (1337–1453). The Knight and his follower are thus an emblem of the great English past; the Squire, between them, is an example of a fashionable young gentleman.

THE CLERGY

CHECK THE BOOK

One place to check on the language of the Prioress's portrait is David Burnley's *Guide to Chaucer's Language*, 1983.

The clerical estate presents a much less worthy trio. The Prioress is a lady to her fingertips; the Monk 'was a lord ful fat and in good poynt' (line 200). The Friar is a libertine, a playboy and a confidence trickster. They are not what they should be.

THE PRIORESS

The Prioress's faults are, however, minor. Like many Prioresses in the Middle Ages and since, she has the manners of the upper class, which the narrator appears to admire greatly, describing them at length. He is also fascinated by her delicious appearance, which is that of a heroine of romance, as is her name. Her tenderness to her dogs, and the ambiguous motto on her rosary, suggest some diversion of interest on the part of one who has dedicated herself as a bride of Christ. Her tale later turns out to be as conventionally pious as her manners are fine. The narrator is taken by her refinement and femininity and the appearance of a romantic sensibility. The sustained ambiguity of her portrait is examined in **Extended commentaries, text 2.**

THE MONK AND THE FRIAR

Luxury has also affected the other two celibates, the manly Monk and the wanton Friar. The Monk, whose name is later given as Don John, and Friar Huberd both have love tokens, like Madame Eglentyne. The Monk's gold pin with a love-knot (lines 196–7) matches the Nun's gold brooch; the Friar carries a stock of pins to give to pretty women (line 234). Those in religious orders should be self-disciplined but all three regular clergy have personal names (unlike the military trio) and all three have love-tokens: an example of the use of significant detail to link portraits. Both men have luxurious tastes and dress expensively. The Friar's corruption, however, goes deeper than the Monk's.

Monks and nuns had been established in the Church for 1,000 years, and their shortcomings, amusingly displayed here, are those of a worldliness and weakness that was familiar to the laity. Senior monks and nuns were commonly the younger brothers and sisters of the lords and ladies they often resembled. The Friars, however, were only two-and-a-half centuries old. Today we might admire the humility of the Franciscan ideal and the intellectual achievements of Dominicans such as Thomas Aquinas, but the immense success of the fraternal orders was resented, as is clear from the amount of satire they attracted. Their activities, and especially their fund-raising activities, impinged more directly on the lives of urban people than had the old religious orders of monks and nuns. With a roving commission to beg, they could pry into every household and get the better of the housewife. The Friar's portrait is longer by ten lines than that of any other pilgrim.

> **? QUESTION** The Prologue has seven clerics, Church officers and associates. Put them in descending moral order, giving your reasons.

The hunting Monk is a familiar caricature and the details of his fine horses, his fur cuffs and his preference for roast swan could be paralleled from the luxuries and temptations of other anti-clerical satire in the Middle Ages. It might be more profitable, then, to focus on details of Chaucer's art rather than on his social criticism. Three techniques used in the portrait are repeated elsewhere. Few of the pilgrims are presented entirely by listing visual details, as in the case of the Yeoman; the chief method, especially in satirical portraits, is to describe with admiration and enthusiasm all those features of which the victim himself is particularly proud. Thus the

The Clergy continued

QUESTION
The poet
Lydgate wrote
that Chaucer
'seide alwey the
beste'. In the
Prologue, can you
distinguish
Chaucer's charity
from his
diplomacy?

Monk's manliness, fine horses, supple boots and diet are remarked on with warm approval. Secondly, the narrator appears to report or echo the words of the pilgrim's most revealing statements. Thus, lines 174–89 virtually report a conversation in which the Monk gives himself away by protesting against the strictness of the old Rule of St Benedict, although, as a Regular, he has bound himself to keep these Rules by a religious vow. However, the pilgrim Chaucer draws further attention to the Monk's laxity by mentioning two other monastic obligations, namely, daily study and manual labour, and crowns the irony by asking how *the world* shall be served. While the established monastic orders provided excellent administrators in secular fields, this was not the intention of their founders, who withdrew from this world in order to prepare for the next. By accepting the Monk's secular role and, in his eagerness to agree, emphasising its (entirely false) premise, Chaucer or his narrator feigns ignorance and creates irony at the extent of the Monk's self-deception or self-forgetfulness.

These two techniques, praising the subject's most inappropriate vices and quoting his idiocies with approval, are part of Chaucer's basic satirical method, which is to allow fools to give themselves away. A third aspect – word-play – is different and elusive, as it relies on an awareness both of historical English and of social history. At line 199 the narrator says the Monk's bald head and jolly face gleamed with good living 'as it had been enoynt'. The monk's head was bald since it had been tonsured in sign of renunciation of manly vanity, and (if he is a priest) had been anointed, not with fat living but with the sacramental oil of Holy Orders. There are still public houses called the Monk's Head or the Merry Monk, with floridly painted inn signs. The satire is not bitter but comical, as the Monk seems to have a stronger idea of what the monastic ideal is not rather than of what it is.

The same ironies are applied more sarcastically to the Friar. He is the most skilful seducer in all the four (celibate) orders (line 211). He kindly arranges marriages – for girls whom he has made pregnant (lines 212–4). He gives an easy penance – in return for a good bribe (lines 223–4). These are examples of vice being praised. Lines 225–30 exemplify the second technique of echoing the Friar's transparent excuses. His plausible patter is again quoted in lines 243–8. There seems to be an indecent *double-entendre* on the word *post* in line 214.

Two further, more poetic, features are exemplified in the portrait of the Friar. One is the use of the rhyming couplet for the purposes of comic anti-climax, as in:

> Ful wel biloved and famulier was he
> With frankeleyns over all in his contree. (lines 215–16)

The first line praises the Friar's gift of friendly intimacy and raises expectations that the object of this brotherly attention will be the deserving poor. The second reveals that he prefers the society of people who can entertain him luxuriously. In lines 223–4, the rhyme *penaunce/pitaunce* is particularly telling. Finally, there is a rare example of a poetic **simile**:

> And in his harpyng, when that he hadde songe
> His eyen twynkled in his heed aryght
> As doon the sterres in the frosty nyght. (lines 265–7)

Most of the images in the Prologue are proverbial; this is more decorative. However, the comparison of the charming Friar's twinkling eyes to the stars is rendered suddenly chilling by the inclusion of *frosty*. The calculating nature of the professional parasite is delicately revealed. It is by these tiny touches that the poet makes his effects, and converts the stereotypes of satire into recognisable people. It is because he speaks of them so sympathetically and admiringly for being what they are, that Chaucer is often regarded as being a humorous and comic writer rather than a reforming satirist.

CONTEXT

London, like the burgher cities of the Low Countries, the Rhine and Northern Italy, was a major trading and financial centre.

PROFESSIONALS

THE MERCHANT

The Merchant is, perhaps symbolically, placed first in this group of burghers.

After the lavishness of the Friar's description, the Merchant's is short and understated. Yet every seemingly off-hand line tells us more about this man of substance: four on his good clothes; four on his talk, boastful and fearful by turns; five on his shady financial dealing; an inconclusive final couplet.

Chaucer's pretended guilelessness is now so well established that we expect him to be impressed by anyone. He prattles on, full of empty phrases like 'ful well', 'for anything', 'For sothe'. In the last couplet he reinforces 'for sothe' with 'sooth to sey', and artlessly repeats 'worthy man' from line 279. We remember that Chaucer, according to Lydgate, 'seyde alwey the beste'. Yet the poet conveys to us that even his social **persona** finds the Merchant rather hard work: he was worthy (that is, he seemed a sound man) but chose not to give his name. The Merchant may have travelled in company for safety's sake. His self-importance about his business is self-defeating, since his confidential remark to the narrator that no-one knew he was in debt (line 280) is gossiped to the whole world. We now appreciate the force of lines 31–2: 'So hadde I spoken with hem everichon / That I was of hir felaweship anon.'

THE CLERK

The Clerk is a contrast to the Merchant, as the Squire was to the Knight. The Merchant is worldly, the Clerk unworldly, and this shows in every detail of their clothes, mounts, interests and conversation. The man of money booms his business; the philosopher is crisp and instructive. The portraits are linked by the word *sownynge* (lines 275, 307). Chaucer's man-of-the-world persona is amused by the Clerk's unworldliness, and jokes about this philosopher who has no gold. But the writer speaks warmly about the Clerk's love of books, his true piety and his elevated, economical speech. The difference between the poet's values and those of his social persona is evident.

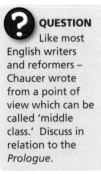

QUESTION
Like most English writers and reformers – Chaucer wrote from a point of view which can be called 'middle class.' Discuss in relation to the *Prologue*.

THE SERGEANT OF THE LAW

The Sergeant is another impressively learned man, but with plenty of gold in his coffer. He applies his skills to personal enrichment, in further contrast to the Oxford cleric. It can be seen now that the placing of the Clerk's portrait was for dramatic and moral contrast, not for social precedence. The theme of greed is forced into prominence by this sandwiching of the spiritual man between the men of substance. (The lawyer may be the more substantial, since he turns his fees and robes into land.)

The manner and conversation of the three men are again compared. The lawyer's words seemed worthy *of* reverence (lines 312–3), whereas the Clerk's few words were spoken *with* reverence. The Clerk's wisdom is seen in the 'hy sentence' and 'moral virtue' of his speech; the Sergeant's words seemed wise, but his expertise has brought him wariness and discretion – canny prudence rather than wisdom. His *writyng* (line 326) was more reliable than his word, for writing secured title to land. A distrust of lawyers shows in the use of the word *semed* (line 322 – 'And yet he semed bisier than he was') repeated from line 313. The simplicity of line 322 makes it as effective today as it was 600 years ago, despite all the changes in the language.

QUESTION
Does Chaucer have a uniform attitude to those who profess to serve God, or the common good, rather than themselves?

THE FRANKLIN

The companion of the purchaser of land is a land-holder. The Franklin's assured social standing exempts him from the moneymaking that affects other pilgrims, but in his Epicureanism (see below – **The Doctor of Physic**) he shows the same gusto in self-gratification that makes even the most imperfect pilgrim so entertaining. The Franklin's philosophy and style of life are picturesquely described, with poetic figures (lines 332, 345–6, 358). The final lines list the important offices that had brought him into contact with the Sergeant.

The picture of country hospitality is the first of many in English, done with a Chaucerian combination of cordiality, freshness, slight hyperbole and affectionate mockery, as in:

Ful many a fat partrich hadde he in muwe,
And many a breem and many a luce in stuwe. (lines 349–50)

As often in Chaucer, it is at the rhyme that the wit becomes
apparent:

Whit was his berd as is a dayesye.
Of his complexioun he was sangwyn.
Wel loved he by the morwe a sop in wyn. (lines 332–4)

The simple, factual lines succeed each other without a hint of
malice, yet the rhyming of *sangwyn* with *wyn* suggests that the
wine may have helped the blood in producing the Franklin's ruddy
complexion. This kind of identical rhyme was admired. The good
living of the Franklin is not regarded too critically, if one can go by
the innocence of the comparisons to the daisy and morning milk.

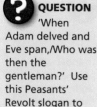

QUESTION
'When
Adam delved and
Eve span,/Who was
then the
gentleman?' Use
this Peasants'
Revolt slogan to
discuss social
hierarchy in the
General Prologue.

THE GUILDSMEN

The absence of a link between the Franklin and the Guildsmen
contributes to the unpremeditated air of Chaucer's report on his
fellow pilgrims. The Guildsmen are perhaps the least interesting
members of the pilgrimage, partly because they are not
individualised (none of them tells a tale), partly because they are the
object of a satire that is rather predictable. The guilds, though their
members were artisans, were wealthy enough to ignore the
sumptuary laws. Sumptuary law prescribed the particular type of
dress which was to be worn by each class and trade (see note to line
366). Aldermen, and more especially their wives, have been an easy
target for satire ever since the Middle Ages. Their simple pride in
their wealth and their wives' social pretensions amuse Chaucer – as
is shown in the superb **hyperbole** of *roialliche* in the last line, an
example of the poet's intuitive understanding of the social fantasies
of the worthy matrons. Another irony is the approval given by the
narrator to this social pride in externals and status in line 375.

THE COOK

The Guildsmen have their own cook, a sign of affluence and
pretension. Like all the pilgrims, the Cook is the best of his kind,
and Chaucer delights as usual in giving us all the special language of

this particular art. But despite the narrator's enthusiasm, his dishes sound ordinary enough, compared with the fare expected of the Franklin's cook. Is the *mormal* on his shin the result of his connoisseurship of London's ale? This is the sort of question prompted by the straightfaced (repulsive) juxtaposition of the *mormal* and *blankmanger*. As with the Franklin's *sangwyn* complexion, we cannot be sure, but that Chaucer enjoyed such urbane ironies is certain. His background would also have given him a thorough knowledge of the catering trade.

? QUESTION
Comment on how Chaucer's portraits blend stock types with apparently casual detail.

THE SHIPMAN

The same inside knowledge informs the portrait of the Shipman. The first eight lines give us a picturesque sailor, suntanned, comically unfamiliar with horses. The tenth contains a wonderfully unexpected turn:

> Ful many a draughte of wyn had he ydrawe
> Fro Burdeux-ward, whil that the chapman sleep. (lines 396–7)

The sentence is innocent until the last two words deliver the sting in its tail. It turns out that the Shipman has not innocently 'carried many cargoes' while the merchants slept; rather he had secretly 'drunk copious draughts' of their wine. Chaucer, a vintner's son, repays a professional grudge. We now hear of the Shipman's method of dealing with captives, and the dagger of lines 392–3 begins to look more dangerous. The vivid glimpse of the Shipman's callousness fades, however, under the lengthy catalogue of his impressive professional skills, ending in a circumstantial point added as an afterthought, like the comment on the Cook's ability with blankmanger. Such details allow us to believe that Chaucer is recalling what the man had told him.

THE DOCTOR OF PHYSIC

The theme of food and drink, raised with the Prioress and the Monk and dominating the portrait of the Franklin, continues with the Doctor of Physic. First, however, we hear of his professional prowess – the most encyclopedic of all these lists of authorities and terms of art, a medieval convention which Chaucer seems particularly to have enjoyed. Like the Knight, he is a 'verray, parfit'

example of his kind, but in his case this involves conspiracy with
the apothecary against the patient – an ancient complaint against
doctors. After he has displayed to us his improbably vast Arabic
knowledge, we come to his diet. As we might expect from the best
doctor in the world (line 412), his diet is moderate:

> But of greet norissyng and digestible.
> His studie was but litel on the Bible. (lines 437–8)

CONTEXT

In 1348–49 the
Black Death killed
about a third of
the population of
England, returning
several times
during Chaucer's
life.

The description moves immediately to his (costly) dress, but the
one-liner about the Doctor's neglect of the Bible is a shrewd thrust,
as unexpected as the Shipman's nocturnal thieving. The rhyme is
particularly clever, pointedly contrasting the Doctor's scrupulous
and learned care for his body with his neglect of his soul. The last
two couplets destroy the Doctor's character: to him the Black
Death (the bubonic plague, for which there was no cure) has
brought gold, gold which he is not going to pass on to others.
Meanness was a vice even more unpopular in the Middle Ages than
it is now. All his learning merely makes him rich. The impressive
edifice is inhabited by a miser.

THE WIFE OF BATH

The liveliness of the Wife of Bath, one of Chaucer's most famous
characters, comes as a relief. Her portrait is enormously amplified
later on by the immensely long preamble to her tale, where she
indulges in unrestrained autobiography. Her garrulous tongue is
only hinted at in line 474. In her Prologue she explains her five
husbands, and also two apparently inconsequential points of the
portrait – her deafness (line 446) and the connection between her
wandering and her teeth (lines 467–8). The illogicality of the
narrator's *but* in line 446 is characteristic of him – she was a good
woman but unfortunately rather deaf. The deafness is, however, a
significant detail, the result of a blow on the ear from her fifth
husband. He had been reading to her from an encyclopedic work
on the faults of women, when she knocked him into the fire and
tore three leaves from his book; he struck her on the ear, but was so
alarmed when she fainted that she was able to make him promise to
give her sovereignty in the marriage. In medieval theory and law,
biblical in origin, the man is the head of the woman, and should be
obeyed. The Wife, however, is not at all receptive to this doctrine,

and her deafness is **symbolic** of this unwillingness to listen.
Physical characteristics in these portraits often have a moral import.
Thus the Wife explains in her Prologue:

> Gat-tothed I was, and that bicam me weel:
> I hadde the prente of seinte Venus seel.
> (I was gate-toothed, which became me well: I had the print of St
> Venus's seal.) (*Wife of Bath's Prologue*, lines 603–4)

Medieval students of physiology held that to have teeth widely
spaced (gate-toothed) was a sign of boldness, falseness, gluttony
and lasciviousness; the Wife, born under Venus (who was no saint),
regards it as confirming her venereal nature. The Wife's 'gate' teeth
gave her many opportunities to wander off the road. It is
characteristic of Chaucer that these two apparently irrelevant
physical details are made to seem even more casual by being
qualified by, 'and that was scathe' and 'soothly for to seye' – the
fill-in or tag phrases of his chatty narrative.

The Wife's portrait begins with a standard feature of the dreadful
women whom clerks (and comic writers) in the Middle Ages liked
to caricature. She is self-important and vain (lines 449–52) in
exactly the same way as the wives of the Guildsmen (lines 376–8).
This liking for display is cleverly combined by Chaucer with her
profession (cloth-making); and her vanity in church (a scandal to
clerics) is treated with the hyperbole of *roialliche* (line 378), but
here carried to magnificent heights of absurdity. The Church
required that at Mass women should cover their heads, lest their
hair distract the men. The Wife's coverchiefs, of her own
manufacture, weigh ten pound, over two kilos (or so it is reported).
Her stockings are scarlet and tight-laced, and her shoes are 'moyste
and newe'. She is thus the scarlet woman, flaunting her wares,
whom the preachers against female vanity loved to hate. But – and
this is very Chaucerian – she is both sexually attractive and at the
same time ridiculously overdressed. Her face is bold and red (the
colour of Mars) but also *fair* (comely).

> **QUESTION**
> Compare
> and contrast the
> portraits of the
> Prioress and the
> Wife of Bath.

The Wife turns out to be the monster of anti-feminist comedy –
aggressive, nagging, gossiping, lustful, vain, wasteful, domineering.
Yet she is not unattractive. She is also more human than any

stereotype, and many find her lovable in her overflowing vanity. In the General Prologue, she is primarily a comic figure. The touches of hyperbole at the beginning of her portrait are followed by a series of hints that her amorous adventures have been epically excessive. Apart from her five husbands and other youthful company we are told that she had 'passed many a straunge strem' (line 464) and knew a lot about 'wandrynge by the weye' (line 466). These nudges and winks from Chaucer are continued in the details of her easy riding, her spurs, and finally:

> Of remedies of love she knew per chaunce
> For she koude of that art the olde daunce. (lines 475–6)

The *remedies* and *olde daunce* do not suggest virtue. All in all, she is quite a contrast to the chastity, modesty and refinement of the Prioress.

www. CHECK THE NET
All the miniature portraits in the Ellesmere manuscript are well reproduced at http://www.liu.edu/cwis/cwp/library/sc/chaucer/chaucer.htm

Finally, the Wife's portrait contains symbolic details of a sort that appears increasingly in the satirical portraits of the lower characters. Thus, the redness of her face, her hat as broad as a shield and her sharp spurs all suggest her martial qualities. In the miniature portrait of her in the Ellesmere Manuscript she carries a whip to beat her husbands.

GOOD MEN

THE PARSON AND THE PLOUGHMAN

The Parson is 'a good man' but good in a different way from the 'good Wife'. The Wife is *worthy:* she has had five husbands. The Merchant is *worthy;* and the Manciple is *gentil.* Yet these adjectives have also been applied to the Knight. We are invited to discriminate between moral worth and social worth. Chaucer points out that the poor Parson is spiritually rich, and does not call him 'a good felawe'. He is prepared to rebuke obstinate sinners.

The goodness of the Parson and the Ploughman sets them apart from the social world through which we have been descending. They are described in terms of their virtues rather than their physical appearance, diet or tastes. Idealists are thus described idealistically, just as materialists have been described in material terms. The contrast is absolute. Both brothers' characters are formed directly upon the ideals of the Church and the Gospel. Unlike the professionals and their servants, and unlike many clerics, they give rather than take, they love God and their neighbour, work hard for others, and are humble. Although such men were as rare as saints, their ideals are clearly believed in. There is energy as well as piety in both descriptions, and they are made persuasive by the same colloquial actuality that animates the other portraits. The Parson was 'loth … to cursen' (line 486), he caught the words out of the gospel, he ran not to London, his speech was not 'daungerous ne digne' (line 517). The Ploughman was 'a trewe swynkere' (line 531) and loved God 'thogh him gamed or smerte' (line 532). The Parson is developed beyond an ideal, and if Knight, Parson and Ploughman represent medieval social ideals, the Parson is the most fully realised. A 'noble example', he is also a real village priest: if the Ploughman carts dung, it is the Parson who speaks of *a shiten shepherd*. Chaucer further applies the **metaphor** of *clennesse* to gold and to the mire which encumbers the sheep. Christ's pastoral parables are made at home in the land of England. This shepherd is benign (lines 483, 518):

> To drawen folk to hevene by fairnesse,
> By good ensample, this was his bisynesse. (lines 519–20)

He is not overscrupulous, but is prepared to snub obstinacy when necessary – as he does the Host at the end of the pilgrimage.

> **CONTEXT**
>
> Life in Chaucer's England was physical. Most people worked the land and slept several to a bed.

STEWARDS

The last six pilgrims are introduced as a group. What have they in common? All except Chaucer are dishonest stewards who defraud those they serve, and abuse positions of trust. They are criticised with a less friendly irony.

THE MILLER

There was broad comedy in the portrait of the Wife of Bath, not without mild vulgarity. The Miller, however, is a grotesque figure, coarse and menacing. His description is unprecedentedly physical, partly because his brutal strength is the key to his character (he is a bully) and partly because of the satirical tradition of caricaturing vice as gross and beastly. A powerful physical presence is immediately suggested, and there follow sundry unattractive details of his features, with a final mixture of remarks on his habits and dress. Closer attention to the portrait, however, transforms this 'realistic' physical portrait into a moral emblem.

Discord is suggested by wrestling, door-smashing, weapons and *jangling* (line 560). A procession led by bagpipes may not prove harmonious. Even the Miller's profession involves breaking and crushing. Bestial affinities are suggested by the brawn, bones, ram, sow, fox, and sow's ears (out of which, according to the old English proverb, silk purses cannot be made). The hairs on the wart on the top of his nose are red, as are his beard and his huge mouth, whereas his nostrils are black. These last details seem sinister, even hellish: the Devil's mouth is portrayed in medieval painting as the gaping mouth of a furnace. The Miller's bullying brutality makes more impression than his dishonesty or his dirty mind.

THE MANCIPLE

The Manciple, by contrast, is *gentil,* but a thief of others' food, like the Miller, if more discreetly. Discretion and prudence are ironically described as *wise* in line 569 and *wisdom* in line 575. In this wise buying, the Manciple emulates the wise purchasing of the Sergeant of the Law (line 318). The narrator is amused by seeing the legal defrauders legally defrauded by their uneducated servant, as becomes clear with the last line. The Manciple is not individualised – he is a faceless man.

THE REEVE

The Reeve is mean in every sense. He is scrawny, unlike the Miller, and angry, unlike the Manciple. In other respects he resembles the Manciple, whose lines 579–86 also apply to the Reeve: he cheats his lord in a way that the lord cannot detect. He is also like the Miller in that he oppresses those below him (lines 603–5). Millers were the natural enemies of reeves and of carpenters, and the Reeve is a carpenter too. They ride at opposite ends of the pilgrimage.

The three dishonest stewards are thus closely linked by similarities and contrasts. The antipathy of the Miller and the Reeve prepares

CHECK THE BOOK

The Bible of the Middle Ages was the Latin Vulgate, from which the closest English translation of the New Testament was made at Rheims in 1582. Jesus told parables about dishonest stewards, e.g. Matthew 18: 23.

us for their tales, which immediately follow and contrast with the Knight's and set in motion the dramatic conflicts which animate the *Tales* thereafter. Yet the Reeve's portrait has touches rich beyond the necessities of any future dramas. There are few more varied passages in the Prologue than lines 603–12. The Reeve's professional skills become sinister in line 605, and the deathly fear in which he is held casts an ironic light upon the pastoral setting of his house: 'With grene trees yshadwed was his place' (line 607), although green was not always a good colour in medieval lore. His lord's kindness to him and his own cruelty to his inferiors echoes several of Jesus's parables. But the Reeve's cunning manipulation of his lord is a Chaucerian theme: the Reeve takes pleasure in being thanked by his victim (line 612). This expresses the age's disgust at hypocrisy, and a Gothic taste for dramatic reversal. One of Chaucer's most famous lines is 'The smylere with the knyf under the cloke' (Knight's Tale, line 1998).

ECCLESIASTICAL VILLAINS

Last come the precious pair of ecclesiastical villains whom even the charitable Chaucer, who can hate the sin but love the sinner, derides.

THE SUMMONER

The Summoner is the simpler of the two: a lecher, a drunkard, a corrupt officer of the law, easily bribed by a drink from a fellow-criminal; demanding bribes from those who prefer their purses to their souls; corrupting the young. The opinion that a writ of imprisonment (because it costs money) is worse than an excommunication is the Summoner's. Chaucer does not as a rule openly attribute opinions to his characters but rather seems to report them. The Summoner, like the Pardoner, does not believe in what he does. Sarcasm rather than irony is the note, as in the comments on the Summoner's Latin (lines 637–46) and his kindness (lines 647–65). Lechery is his ruling passion: his face is *fyr-reed* (line 624) and he is *hoot* (line 626). This is shown by his facial acne and his love of hot foods and strong drink. For him, *wyn* rhymes with *Latyn* (line 638) and *concubyn* (line 650). Bread and wine appear in the last couplet, and it may be that, as in the Pardoner's Tale, these are connected with the inability of the sinner to partake of communion. Excommunication was the ultimate penalty of the court the Summoner served.

> **CONTEXT**
>
> Excommunication debarred the person punished from receiving Christ in the Eucharist.

Ecclesiastical villains continued

THE PARDONER

The Pardoner is cleverer sillier and more corrupt than the cunning but stupid Summoner. He sings alto to the Summoner's bass, and he is physically a eunuch, an incomplete man (line 691). This explains not just his affected hairstyle, but his carrying the (false) pardons or bulls in his lap as a compensating source of potency. His lack of masculinity symbolises the falsity and inefficacy of what he sells.

The Pardoner has false relics, which fool the ignorant country folk into giving him money which should go to the parish priest. He preaches well, as he later explains, because his takings depend upon it. The Pardoner's own Prologue and Tale dramatically illustrate in detail how he uses his relics, how he preaches and tells a story, and how he blackmails the guilty and ignorant into buying his pardons. The Host, however, exposes the sterile nature of the Pardoner's false bulls from Rome, and exposes him also as a eunuch. The Pardoner is contemptible because he defrauds the poor, like a crooked insurance salesman, but he is doubly unwelcome on the pilgrimage, because he usurps the function of the Parson. Pardoners could not pardon sins, nor were they licensed to preach. This Pardoner was probably not a cleric, did not come from Rome, sold false pardons and, as his Tale shows, did not believe in the pardons he professed to sell. He was thus a complete fraud. By a significant irony, the theme of his sermon is '*Radix malorum est cupiditas*' ('the love of money is the root of all evils'). He is not a pilgrim but a dangerous parasite, a wolf in sheep's clothing. Hence he is symbolically made a eunuch of repugnant appearance – a fit partner for the corrupt ecclesiastical policeman who aids and abets him. The Pardoner, like the Wife of Bath, is a character developed much more fully in his Prologue.

> **CONTEXT**
>
> In the 1520s Martin Luther attacked the sale of pardons to fund the building of Michaelangelo's Basilica over the tomb of St Peter in Rome.

From this review of the portraits emerge the themes of avarice and human self-ignorance. Gratitude and penitence, which in the end of the Tales the Parson starkly recalls to the minds of the pilgrims, do not seem to be uppermost in the minds of most of the pilgrims nor of the Host. But only the Pardoner is there simply to make money out of the others. The loathing felt for the Pardoner's absolute falsity, and the fervour of the Parson's portrait, imply faith.

Chaucer detests the mercenary and loves the true shepherd (line 514). Toward those clerics who fall between the two – the Nun, Monk and Friar – he is subtly, broadly or keenly satirical. In many of the other portraits his comic vision is mediated by means of an irony that allows much flexibility in interpretation.

What conclusions about Chaucer's view of his society can be drawn from the Prologue portraits? It was not, of course, Chaucer's purpose to present an analysis of society for the modern historian, but to introduce a work of fiction. The portraits of the pilgrims are presented through the medium of a very impressionable social persona whose values do not always represent the author's deeper views. Thus, Chaucer says that he agrees that the Monk is right to do no work (lines 186–8), but he also makes us doubt the truth of this. His own views are hard to ascertain, except at the extremes. It is clear that we are to admire the Knight, Parson and Ploughman, but not the Summoner or the Pardoner. Attitudes to the pilgrims in between vary from indulgence (the Squire), to irony (the Doctor) and satire. Such views were not new, but their indirect and humorous method of delivery is, and the effect is both more engaging and thought-provoking than direct satire.

THE ROAD TO CANTERBURY

The remainder of the Prologue looks forward to the tale-telling competition and the pilgrimage. After the detail of the portraits, Chaucer reestablishes his **persona** as an amiable bumbler, confiding to the audience: 'My wit is short, ye may well understonde' (line 746). Humility is the poet's favourite guise.

THE HOST

The Host recreates the merry cheer which was a medieval social ideal. Having feasted the pilgrims (and received payment), he proposes a game which will increase their mirth – and cost them nothing (line 668). In fact it is to cost all but one of them the price of another supper at the Tabard on their return. The Host, as president of the game, will be able to play the part of 'a marchal in an halle' (line 752) for which his physique and talents fit him well. He thus secures custom, profit for himself, diversion and what

CHECK THE BOOK

A handy collection of articles is *The General Prologue to the Canterbury Tales*, ed H. Bloom, 1991.

today might be called an ego-trip. While we note the Host's shrewdness and dexterity in stage-managing this takeover, we are also impressed by his good humour. He captures the good will of the pilgrims by flattery and exuberance and with a masterly sales talk. Had the pilgrimage gone according to the Host's plan, he would have had 'a thank, and yet a cote and hood' (line 612), like the Reeve. Unlike the Reeve, however, he seems a good fellow.

As referee of the tale-telling game, the Host speaks in nearly all of the links between the tales which follow the Prologue. After the Knight's Tale, the Host's authority is challenged by the Miller, and it becomes clear that Harry Bailly is unable to control this quarrelsome drunkard; who gleefully adds insult to his insubordination by blaming his drunken state on the quality of the ale supplied at the Tabard on the previous evening. Later we hear the Host confess that he is scared of his wife's tongue. So the masculine commander of the game, 'oure aller cok', who leads 'us' all out of town in line 823, turns out to be a hen-pecked husband. Our initial impression of Harry Bailly as a good-humoured fellow is also modified as his reactions to various of the tales later show him at different points to be impatient, ignorant, patronising, soft-hearted, thin-skinned, or easily bored – as by Chaucer's own story of Sir Thopas. Finally, with Canterbury in sight, the Host address the Parson rather too flippantly, and is put in his place by having to listen to the Parson's 'merry tale in prose', (Parson's Prologue, line 46) a detailed catalogue of the Seven Deadly Sins and their many branches. For a similar error he had earlier been lectured by Chaucer in the tale of Melibeus and Prudence. The Host's role, largely a comic one, is as the average man in the audience.

One consequence of the Host's cheery ultimatum is that the pilgrimage is transformed, without our noticing it, into a party game. The pilgrim narrator enjoys good company, and may have no objection, but not all the pilgrims may have been equally happy with the promise into which they had innocently been hustled – the Prioress, the Parson, the Miller and the Pardoner might all have different objections. But the Host manages it so that we hear nothing of objections, but only of ease, mirth, merriment, disport, comfort, wine and ale. Also that anyone who disobeys him will have to pay the expenses of the others, and that the prize supper

? **QUESTION**
The Host was 'oure aller cok'. How many times in the *Prologue* are humans compared with animals?

will be at a fixed price. It is notable, however, that in the arrangements for the competition (lines 790–801), the tales are to be 'of aventures that whilom han bifalle' – the Host's idea of a story – but that the prize will go to him who tells 'tales of best sentence and moost solaas', which is quite another idea, perhaps more like the poet's own.

The Host is at this point an unknown quantity. Like many of the pilgrims, he later turns out to be a professional who is neither as innocent nor as happy as he at first appears. His original description tells us less than his later behaviour, but even this remains finally elusive. *The Canterbury Tales* has already begun to develop on dramatic lines quite different from the static descriptions we have passed through. Our guides, Chaucer as narrator and the Host as master of the game, are both unpredictable.

CHECK THE BOOK

G.K.Chesterton's *Chaucer*, 1932, is a stimulating introduction to medieval thinking as well as to Chaucer.

The setting-out at dawn has narrative verve. The manly Host leads forth his flock at a quiet pace, sternly reminds them of their oaths of obedience, and, while the horses are watered, bids the pilgrims draw. He politely invites the senior gentleman and lady present to draw, but jokingly presses the serious Clerk to submit himself also to the dominion of chance; and rounds up the others.

It seems that the Host may have fixed the cut so that the Knight gets the short straw. The narrator is delighted by this fortunate turn of events. The Host has thus at the outset involved the most honoured and authoritative of the pilgrims. The Knight proves to be a good sport, and jovially agrees to tell the first tale. The pilgrimage is forgotten and the game has begun.

CHRISTIAN COMEDY

Chaucer is a comic writer with a rich sense of humanity, yet *The Canterbury Tales* is more than a human comedy: it is, as Dryden said, 'God's plenty.' Comedy in a simple medieval sense of the word means a story with a happy ending. At the end of his great *Troilus and Criseyde* (which he calls 'litel myn tragedye'), Chaucer prays that God will send him the ability to try his hand in 'some comedye'. Dante (1265–1321) had entitled his pilgrimage through Hell and Purgatory to Heaven the *Commedia*, not because it was humorous but because it ends in a happier state than it began. Chaucer's *Tales* are a large and varied work, where the part obscures the whole, where we shift between tellers and their tales, and where the design is not completed. However, the pilgrimage is more than a device. The Parson, 'a good man of religioun' (line 477), tells the last tale, late in the evening as the shadows are lengthening. It is an uncompromising treatise on the necessity for repentance, and comes as a shock. In retrospect, after the Knight's 'noble storie' (Miller's Prologue, line 3111), the pleasant pilgrimage can be seen to have declined into a comic, quarrelsome, blasphemous and sometimes brutal chaos, the lowest point of which is the Cook's drunken fall from his horse into the slough. As the pilgrims near Canterbury, their fallibility and confusion become manifest. The Parson asks Jesus for his grace: 'To shewe yow the wey, in this viage, / Of thilke parfit glorious pilgrymage, / That highte Jerusalem celestial' (Parson's Prologue, lines 49–51).

Here the Parson is speaking **allegorically**: the way to the heavenly Jerusalem is by the path of repentance – a straight and narrow way unlike the broad and easy road to Canterbury. There are many glimpses, hints and reminders of this 'high way' among the more sinful as well as the more pious tales. Nevertheless, despite the comic delight in and understanding of human self-delusion, and despite all its abounding charity towards the sinner, Chaucer's human world is organised by the Christian hatred of sin made explicit only in the Parson's Tale.

CONTEXT

Among the historical senses of 'Humanist' are (1) student of classical literature; (2) one who values humanity; (3) atheist.

The General Prologue is so sunny, sane, earthly and human that it may be necessary to emphasise that although Chaucer has been called the first humanist in English literature and the first realist in portraying personal and social relations, he remains also a medieval Christian in his sense of the impermanence of this human life which seems so real. This appears only obliquely in the Prologue, which is largely static, with little dramatic interaction between the characters, but the claims of Christ colour the opening and the portraits of the Knight, Parson and Ploughman.

The perennial Christian philosophy is economically expressed outside the *Tales* in the poem of Chaucer's which appears most often in manuscripts, *Truth,* or the *Balade de Bon Conseyl.* Italicised final *-e* is to be sounded.

Flee fro the prees, and dwelle with sothfastnesse,
Suffyce unto thy good, though it be smal;
For hord hath hate, and climbing tikelnesse,
Prees hath envye, and wele blent overal;
Savour no more than thee bihove shal;   5
Reule wel thyself, that other folk canst rede;
And trouthe thee shal delivere, it is no drede.

Tempest thee noght al croked to redresse,
In trust of hir that turneth as a bal:
Gret reste stant in litel besinesse;   10
Be war also to sporne ayeyns an al;
Stryve not, as doth the crokke with the wal.
Daunte thyself, that dauntest otheres dede;
And trouthe thee shal delivere, it is no drede.

That thee is sent, receyve in buxumnesse;   15
The wrastling for this world axeth a fal.
Her is non hoom, her nis but wildernesse:
Forth, pilgrim, forth! Forth, beste, out of thy stal!
Know thy contree, look up, thank God of al;
Hold the heye wey, and lat thy gost thee lede;   20
And trouthe thee shal delivere, it is no drede.

**CHECK
THE BOOK**
*The Consolation of
Philosophy* by
Boethius (c. 480-
524), translated by
King Alfred the
Great, Chaucer and
Queen Elizabeth I, is
also translated by
V E Watts in
Penguin Classics
(1969).

This can be literally rendered:

Leave the throng of Court and make your home with Truth;
content yourself with what you have, though it be slender. For
hoarding is attended by hatred and worldly preferment by
precariousness; the Court is full of envy, and success quite blinds
its possessor. Relish no more than what shall become you;
govern yourself well, that you may counsel others; and Truth
shall most certainly deliver you.

Do not torment yourself to reform all that is amiss, putting
your trust in her who turns like a ball [Fortune]. Great peace is
to be found in little business; beware also of kicking against the
pricks; do not strive as does the pot against the wall. Tame
yourself, you who tame the actions of others, and Truth shall
most certainly deliver you.

Accept with a good will what is sent you: wrestling for this world asks for a fall. There is no home here; here is nothing but a wilderness: out, pilgrim, out! Out, beast, out of thy stall! Acknowledge your native land – look up, thank God for everything. Stick to the high road and let your spirit lead you; and Truth shall assuredly deliver you.

This advice comes from a man who seems quite at home in this world. It may be that Chaucer himself had discovered that 'The wrastling for this world axeth a fal' (line 16). But the philosophy is traditional – it has been described as a resumé of the *Consolation of Philosophy* of Boethius, one of the most popular and influential books of the Middle Ages, and a work which Chaucer translated. The *Consolation* is itself a resumé of Stoic and Platonic thinking on the Contempt of the World, as it was called in Christian tradition. Stoicism was a widespread classical philosophical and ethical system of thought centred on obedience to natural law. Plato (*c.*429–347BC) taught that the world of physical appearances and events is unreal. Chaucer's Bon Conseyl, or Good Advice, is to scorn the rewards of this world in order to earn those of the next, which is the homeland of the soul: 'Know thy contree' (line 18). The truth which shall set free the friend to whom the poem is written is the truth of St John's Gospel 8:32: 'Ye shall know the truth, and the truth shall make you free'. The philosophy of *Truth* is a synthesis of classical and Christian moral thought, in which biblical allusions mingle with classical maxims in a proverbial style which may surprise us if we think of the Middle Ages as unfamiliar with classical tradition. The Sermon on the Mount of line 2 and the conversion of Saul (line 11) combine quite happily with Fortune (line 9), a classical goddess unknown to the Bible. The God who is to be thanked (line 19) is the God of Christian revelation, but the sentiments of the first two stanzas of the poem would be familiar to an educated Roman pagan. The fundamental image of the poem is of life as a pilgrimage – a medieval image but not necessarily an ascetic one, as can be seen in the homely and humorous image of the pilgrim as a beast (line 18) to be led by its soul, as a cow is by the cowherd.

Truth can serve as a mini-introduction to the General Prologue, not only because it is a summary of the moral commonplaces of the age, but because it presents the human being as a pilgrim (from Latin *peregrinus*, wanderer). The famous first paragraph of the Prologue is full of classical mythology and the Middle Eastern astronomy of the Zodiac, and also of the natural history of a scientific sort, which places Nature (line 11) in an apparently sovereign position. Yet the sentence ends with the simple piety of the English pilgrimage to Canterbury. It would be equally mistaken to ignore either the naturalism of the introduction or the supernaturalism of the conclusion. The two are blended in the rich synthesis of *Truth*, and in the same blend of an elevated and a homely style. Medieval Christianity was not the religion only of monks and ascetics: the whole of what we now think of as secular society was included in the Incarnation, as was the natural world of bird and 'holt and heeth' (line 6). The spring which keeps the birds awake all night also moves folks to go on pilgrimage to thank the saint who has interceded for them when they were sick. The poet is at home in the physical world which he celebrates, a world which, as he reminds us, we must sooner or later leave behind.

VARIETY AND UNITY

The Canterbury Tales combines in a simple narrative many varied and dramatic subjects of human interest, from the loftiest to the lowest. Factors unifying its very diverse materials include:

(1) The narrative **frame-stories** of the pilgrimage and tale-telling;

(2) The role of the Host as master of ceremonies;

(3) The personality and voice of the narrator, Chaucer the poet and pilgrim;

(4) The dramatic interplay between the characters of the pilgrims, either because their values differ – the Miller's bawdy mocks the Knight's idealism – or because they are professional rivals – the Friar and the Summoner, rival parasites upon the laity, tell tales against each other; as do the Miller and the Reeve;

(5) Intellectual debate, for example on the subject of authority in marriage, the theme of the Wife's Tale and the Clerk's Tale;

(6) An underlying Christian humanism.

> **CONTEXT**
>
> Much of the learning of the ancient world was absorbed by Greek Christians and passed by Syrian Christians to their Muslim conquerors, and so, via Spain, to Western Europe.

The fourth and fifth of these factors do not come out in the Prologue, which introduces the first and second. The third and sixth may be examined in a discussion of the strategy of the Prologue's three parts: the pilgrimage, the pilgrims, and the tale-telling game. The middle part, the pilgrim portraits, is the most substantial thing in the Prologue, but the way we approach it is considerably affected by the narrative sections which frame it.

STYLE

If *The Canterbury Tales* were written today the Prologue would probably be in prose, although some of the Tales require the artifice of verse. Chaucer's own prose was rudimentary compared with his verse, as can be seen in his, prose Tale of Melibee and the Parson's Tale. The Prologue is written in rhyming **pentameters** and in a direct, colloquial, flexible style. It is spoken aloud by the poet to his audience and purports to record his actual experience. Its verse does not go in for the elevation and use of imagery and allusion which are sometimes thought characteristic of poetry, although the opening is formal and later there is the occasional telling use of **simile**.

The language is clear, rapid, almost transparent. It draws no attention to itself except when the narrator apologises for his inadequacies or uses unusually excessive padding (such as 'for the nonys' and 'soothly for to seye'). Chaucer's expository style in the Prologue is a model of simplicity and unaffected unselfconscious elegance: it gives the illusion of a varied stream of discourse, lively, free from artifice or vulgarity. Although so old, it seems fresh, even naïve at times; any quaintness we may feel is the result of our unfamiliarity with Chaucer's world, for although Chaucer is engaging and can be captivating, he was a civilised, courtly and urbane writer. If his age was simpler in its spirit and technology, it was sophisticated as well as earthy. A naïve customs officer is a contradiction in terms: the naïve narrator is a deliberate pose of Chaucer's.

Some of Chaucer's best lines are off-hand: dead-pan yet deadly. If art is to conceal art, Chaucer's art is to seem artless. Many of the casual reflections of his narrator are tellingly accurate:

And yet he seemed bisier than he was (line 322)

or

But sooth to seyn, I noot how men him calle (line 284)

or

They were adrad of hym as of the deeth (line 605)

This style can do whatever is required of it. This reflects a
familiarity with his public that no subsequent author has
exceeded: Chaucer like Shakespeare was both sophisticated and
popular, but his language is less extravagant than Shakespeare's.
This is partly, but only partly, because members of medieval
society had more in common with each other than did those of
post-Reformation England.

The Prologue is verse rather than poetry. Its most easily
pinpointed quality is its surprisingly crisp rhyming, as in the
self-contained couplet:

He was not pale as a forpyned goost:
A fat swan loved he best of any roost. (lines 205–6)

where the association of the rhyme-words makes an unexpected
contrast, sometimes shrewd, sometimes comical. Or the couplet can
be open, and the sense runs on, sometimes in a surprising direction:

She was so charitable and so pitous
She wolde wepe, if that she saugh a mous
Kaught in a trappe ... (lines 143–4)

Here *mous* defines the Nun's pity as directed towards small
animals, rather than towards people as 'charity' had suggested.
Many of the best rhymes are for the purposes of bathos or ironic
wit, reversing the expectations of the previous line. Particularly
audacious are *digestible/Bible* (lines 437–8), *Bathe/scathe* (lines
445–6), *cloystre/oystre* (lines 181–2), *hoot/goot* (lines 687–8)
and *bledde/fedde/deed/breed* (lines 145–9). Each rhyme is a
witty comment.

CHECK THE BOOK
Alcuin Blamires, *The Canterbury Tales*, 1987, is a useful collection of critical articles.

QUESTION
What proportion of the 429 rhyming couplets in the *Prologue* are 'closed' – ending with a punctuation mark heavier than a comma? Do your findings relate to subject-matter and style?

The element of **hyperbole**, or deliberate exaggeration, seen in many of the images of food, dress or physique, also appears in the spectacular skill with which Chaucer sometimes divides a couplet between two utterly disconnected subjects (and so connects them). This is seen at the end of one portrait and the beginning of the next, as at lines 207–8, 269–70 and 387–8; or in the concluding rhyme of many portraits. It is at the rhymes that we feel the sharpness beneath Chaucer's easy tone.

Whether writing about the Prologue's style or themes, its structure or its social satire, it is best to quote a significant detail, a telling line or even a single word, such as *frosty* (line 268) or *roialliche* (line 378). All generalisations about the Prologue, and especially about Chaucer's attitude to society, sound heavy and dull compared with the lightness of his own words.

PART FOUR

CRITICAL HISTORY

HISTORY OF CRITICAL RECEPTION

As Chaucer has been read for six centuries, this is a very brief sketch. In his lifetime he was hailed as *le grand translateur* by Guillaume de Machaut: 'the great translator', that is, of French poems, including *Le Roman de la Rose*.

FIFTEENTH AND SIXTEENTH CENTURY

None of the 400 references to Chaucer in the official records mentions that he was a poet, but on his death he was acknowledged as a master by fifteenth-century poets, notably Hoccleve and Lydgate. The Scots, Robert Henryson, William Dunbar and Gavin Douglas, regard him as the model of style. *The Canterbury Tales* were printed by William Caxton in 1477 and William Thynne in 1532 and regularly thereafter. Chaucer was always read, but his words became harder to read and his music harder to hear. The first edition to explain how Chaucer's metre worked was Thomas Tyrwhitt's in 1775. At first it was Chaucer's earlier and less realistic work which was admired; he was praised for his wisdom and eloquence. In the sixteenth century Edmund Spenser called Chaucer a 'pure well of English undefyled' and traced English poetic tradition from him. Shakespeare based part of *A Midsummer Night's Dream* on the Knight's Tale and based another play, *Two Noble Kinsmen*, on the same tale. Shakespeare often refers to Chaucer. Thereafter most major English poets, from Milton onwards, allude to Chaucer.

THE SEVENTEENTH CENTURY

At the end of the seventeenth century *The Canterbury Tales* became more popular than the poet's earlier work. It was praised as giving a representation of the human comedy, not of his day only but of all time. The neo-classical poet and critic John Dryden (1631–1700) modernised the *Knight's Tale*, and wrote the first perceptive critical account of Chaucer, in the Preface to his *Fables* (1700). He wrote: 'Tis sufficient to say according to the proverb, that here is God's plenty. We have our forefathers and great-

> **www.** CHECK THE NET
> http://geoffrey chaucer.org offers an Annotated Guide to Online Resources and is a good starting place.

The Seventeenth Century continued

grand-dames all before us, as they were in Chaucer's days; their general characters are still remaining in mankind, and even in England, though they are called by other names... For mankind is ever the same, and nothing lost out of Nature, though everything is altered.' This seems to fit the General Prologue. The first of the Romantic poets, William Blake (1757–1827), completely agreed with Dryden's stress on 'general characters': 'Of Chaucer's characters, as described in *The Canterbury Tales*, some of the names or titles are altered by time, but the characters themselves remain unaltered, and consequently they are the phisiognomies or lineaments of universal life, beyond which Nature never steps.'

THE EIGHTEENTH CENTURY

> **CONTEXT**
>
> The only other medieval English work widely read in later times was Sir Thomas Malory's *Le Morte Darthur* (c.1470). Its tales of Knights and Ladies proved very popular with Victorian readers, poets and artists.

The eighteenth century liked to patronise earlier periods as barbarous and crude. It admired Chaucer's 'realism' and comedy, yet attitudes were divided on the subject of Chaucer's bawdy. The humour of his 'low' characters was frequently found too indecent for polite taste, a verdict shared by Daniel Defoe early in the eighteenth, Lord Byron early in the nineteeth, and G.K.Chesterton early in the twentieth century. Yet Defoe's contemporary, Alexander Pope wrote a 'rude' schoolboy tale in pseudo-Chaucerian English. And, more surprisingly, Dorothy Wordsworth wrote in her journal that on Boxing Day 1801, 'After tea, we sate by the fire comfortably. I read aloud – The Miller's Tale.' In this tale, the Miller treats adultery and farting as equally hilarious. The unmarried Dorothy's choice of text may surprise those who think of the Wordsworths as solemn and sensitive; the audience were her brother William and his fiancée. In *The Prelude*, Wordsworth recalls reading the Reeve's Tale when he was at Cambridge: 'Beside the pleasant Mills of Trompington / I laughed with Chaucer.'

THE NINETEENTH CENTURY

Walter Scott based the description of Robin Hood in his most successful romance, *Ivanhoe*, 1819, upon the description of the Yeoman in the *General Prologue*, and took his descriptions of the Monk in *Ivanhoe* from the *Prologue* and of the tournament from the *Knight's Tale*. Victorian poetry is full of allusions to Chaucer, as is the painting of D.G.Rossetti and other Pre-Raphaelites, and Victorian artists generally, notably Ford Madox Brown and Edward

Burne-Jones. The popular American poet Henry Wadsworth Longfellow wrote *Tales of a Wayside Inn* (1863) in imitation of the *Canterbury Tales*. William Morris printed *The Canterbury Tales* in Gothic type at the Kelmscott Press. Historically, then, English people have taken their idea of English medieval poetry mainly from Chaucer, who was the only medieval poet widely available to readers until Victorian times. Likewise, popular ideas of the life of the Middle Ages have been much influenced by the *Canterbury Tales* and its *Prologue*, though these ideas have often been received in versions embroidered by Walter Scott and by the many historical novels and films which have followed Scott's lead.

Although films and adaptations have been made of the more realistic of the *Tales*, these films rarely try to represent the Prologue itself, since the portrait-gallery of the pilgrims, although highly visual is essentially too static for the moving picture industry. Filmed versions of the Tales get the Pilgrims on the move quickly. More informative on the *Prologue*, therefore, are two pictures made in the Regency period (1810-20) by Thomas Stothard and William Blake. Blake's claim that Stothard had pinched the idea from him is disputed at http://allinsongallery.com.stothard.

 CHECK THE NET
The pictures of Stothard and Blake can be studied at **http://www. allinsongallery.com/ stothard/**

The Victorians preferred the uplifting, the beautiful, the tragic. Matthew Arnold judged that Chaucer, though 'free, shrewd, benignant', lacked the 'high seriousness' found in the greatest literature. John Ruskin said that Chaucer taught the purest theological truth. The Edwardian G.K. Chesterton, in the last general pre-academic book, *Chaucer* (1932), wrote well on his Catholicism and his comedy, but turns aside from the cruder tales which have once more become popular.

MODERN APPROACHES

SCHOLARSHIP

Twentieth-century scholarship was based on Skeat's *Oxford Chaucer* (1894–7), the first full modern edition; there have been several other major editions. In the last 100 years the study of Chaucer has continued in British and American universities, and in

the United States has become an academic industry. The approach
has been editorial, philological, historical and empirical: the
establishment of Chaucer's text, and of the meaning of his words
and his references. Chaucer's texts are currently being re-edited
electronically from the 80-odd manuscripts of the *Tales*.

The General Prologue was sometimes treated as a source-book for
medieval social history. This produced a lot of knowledge, much of it
useful. Scholars discovered a hotel-keeper in Southwark in Chaucer's
day called Harry Bailly, a Cook called Roger, a ship called the
Maudelayne in Dartmouth, and an eminent lawyer called Thomas
Pynchbec (a possible link with the word *pynch* in the portrait of the
Man of Law). This seemed to confirm Chaucer's likeness to the
realistic novelists of the nineteenth century and the documentary
novelists of the twentieth. In Muriel Bowden's *Commentary* (1957)
there is plenty of information about pilgrimages, knights, medieval
occupations, the status of a Franklin, the duties of a Manciple or a
Summoner, the rules of dress for nuns and guildsmen, an outline
of medieval medicine, and how *blankmanger* was made. This
information helped with such matters as the sale of pardons, whether
nuns were allowed to keep dogs, and the Wife of Bath's habit of
wearing coverchiefs on her head on Sundays.

CRITICISM

? QUESTION
It is helpful
to distinguish
between Chaucer
the pilgrim and
Chaucer the poet?

Criticism until the 1960s was led by historical scholarship and tended
to make commonsense assumptions about realism and human
continuity, in the tradition of Dryden's 'Here are our fore-fathers…!'
In the 1960s, the process of interpreting Chaucerian narrative was
influenced by the study of narrative point of view, which had
developed in criticism of the novel since the American novelist
Henry James. A good example is the work of E.T. Donaldson, who
made a still influential distinction between Chaucer the pilgrim and
Chaucer the poet (see **Critical approches, Chaucer and narrative**).
Chaucer began to be thought of as less of a naïve realist and more of
a conscious and rather complicated kind of artist. There was much
good criticism of Chaucer in the 1960s and 1970s.

The most notable post-war book on the Prologue is Jill Mann's
Chaucer and Medieval Estates Satire (1973), which convincingly
relates Chaucer's treatment of the pilgrims to the tradition of

estates satire. She shows how much he owes to this tradition, but
also how he modifies its moralism. She further argues that
Chaucer's fascination with and expressed admiration for
professional skill and technical expertise, irrespective of the ends to
which it is directed, may reflect a moral relativism or indifference.
If we think of the Doctor or Lawyer, or the skills with which the
Friar and the Pardoner defraud simple lay people, this seems
unlikely. But how we read Chaucer's irony is influenced by our
presuppositions. One example of misreading is Terry Jones's
Chaucer's Knight, which saw the portrait of the Knight as wholly
ironic, on the grounds that, as he shows, there were no such ideal
knights to be found in the 1380s, but only mercenaries. Jones could
not take the old ideal seriously and could not believe that Chaucer
did. He mistook the tone of the portrait.

LITERARY THEORY

After 1968, literary theory, largely French but imported *via*
America, dazzled and dazed the commonsense which underlay
British criticism, however intelligent or sophisticated. Believers in
structuralism, post-structuralism, deconstruction, new historicism,
cultural materialism and of psychoanalytic and feminist approaches
challenged the assumptions which had governed interpretation in
medieval texts as in others. The competition between these
theorised approaches has exposed the pretensions of any idea which
claims to control the interpretation of all literary texts. None of
these approaches seems to have had much effect on criticism or
understanding of the Prologue. An old notion, revived by literary
theory, suits Chaucer well: the notion that a text can speak with
more than one voice. This approach, associated with the Russian
critic Bakhtin, emphasises that some texts are not the product of
the author's single voice, and that they are not 'monologic' but
dialogic, allowing the expression of various points of view.

Interpretation of the Prologue depends very much on whether the
focus is on what is conveyed, or on how it is conveyed. In the first
case, the content of the portraits will dominate. In the second, the
question of Chaucer's irony becomes prominent, and (whether or
not we distinguish between the pilgrim and the poet)
interpretations will vary. If the operation of irony is admitted, the
reader has to interpret, and an historical awareness should come

> **CONTEXT**
> Literary theory has
> recently lost most
> of its influence,
> and survives
> principally as a
> cover for attitudes
> which are political
> rather than
> philosophical.

Literary theory continued

QUESTION
What is your own attitude to Christianity? How far does it affect your interpretation of the pilgrims?

into play. Otherwise the reader's attitude to religion, for example, or to social hierarchy, or to the roles then available to women, may then dominate the views taken of the military, clerical and mercantile portraits, generally or individually. From such a process, Chaucer may emerge as a satirist, a reformer, a more or less humorous comic writer, as a more or less devout Catholic, as a sceptic or a cynic, or as some combination of these. The idea that Chaucer was a cynic seems, to the authors of these Notes, untrue to the experience of reading him. On the whole, a focus on content rather than narrative point of view will for most readers be simpler and more enjoyable – as long as it is remembered that Chaucer has a sense of humour.

PART FIVE

BACKGROUND

CHAUCER'S LIFE

Geoffrey Chaucer came from a prosperous family which rose in the world through four successive generations. The Chaucers were originally from France. Geoffrey's grandfather was a wine-merchant importing from France. Geoffrey's father, John, was also a wine-merchant in the Vintry in London, by far England's largest city with a population approaching 50,000. That of Paris was 100,000, and of Baghdad, nearly one million. Here the poet was

CHECK THE BOOK

The best recent scholarly Life is Derek Pearsall's *The Life of Geoffrey Chaucer*, Blackwell, 1992.

Portrait miniature in the Ellesmere Manuscript of *The Canterbury Tales* (c. 1410), showing Chaucer riding along the road to Canterbury. A penner or pencase hangs around his neck, signifying that he is a writer. He points to the beginning of his second tale, *The Tale of Melibee*. Pearsall in his Life has an interesting appendix on the Ellesmere illustrations, from which it appears that this portrait of the poet derives from an earlier one which was not equestrian.

born in 1343–4. John once held minor court office as Butler, and Geoffrey followed him in his career as a 'king's man'. Geoffrey had a sister (or daughter) who became a nun. Both his mother and his father's mother were married three times. Long after his death, his son Thomas became one of the most important men in England.

Geoffrey was made a page to Prince Lionel, Edward III's third son. In his teens he fought in the English army in France, where he was captured; Edward III ransomed him in 1360. He is recorded as visiting Spain in 1366, a year in which he married Philippa Payne de Roet. Philippa's sister was Katherine Swynford, the mistress and later the third wife of John of Gaunt, Edward III's fourth son. In 1367 he began travelling abroad on the King's business. In 1369 he fought in Picardy for John of Gaunt. In 1372 he went to Genoa and Florence on a diplomatic mission and revisited Italy in 1378 on a mission to the Lord of Milan.

CHECK THE BOOK

Helen Cooper's *Oxford Guide to The Canterbury Tales*, 1989, is the best modern commentary.

From 1374 Chaucer's career is well documented, for he became Controller of Customs and Subsidy of Wools, Skins and Hides, England's largest trade. He bought a house over Aldgate, the east gate of the City of London. In 1377 he was allowed a deputy at the Custom House and in 1385 moved to Kent, which he represented in Parliament for three years, and was also a Justice of the Peace. He was Clerk for the King's Works in 1389–90, but retired from public life after being robbed and beaten two or three times in four days.

In his last decade, Chaucer was a royal pensioner and substitute forester of the royal forest of North Petherton in Somerset, an office in which he was confirmed by Henry IV in 1399. In 1400 he took a lease on a house in the garden of Westminster Abbey, but died on 25 October and was buried in a chapel of the Abbey which has since become Poets' Corner.

LITERARY CAREER

English poetry flowered in the reign of Richard II after nearly three centuries' submergence beneath the French tradition. It was a great period of English literature in prose, in drama and especially in narrative verse. Major works include *Piers Plowman*, probably by William Langland (*c.* 1331–99?), and the anonymous *Sir Gawain and the Green Knight*, composed in **alliterative metres** deriving from Old English verse. Chaucer's metre and technique, by contrast, derive from the practice of poets in Romance languages. He wrote in English only, unlike John Gower (1330–1408), a court poet ten years his senior, who wrote in French and Latin also. There were good poets before Chaucer, and he had major contemporaries. But later poets regarded Chaucer as the first great exemplar of modern English verse. He made the French **pentameter** natural in English.

Chaucer's work falls into what have been called his French, Italian and English periods. Before 1378 he followed French traditions, translating some of the famous *Roman de la Rose*. *The Book of the Duchess* (1369), his first original work, imitates French allegorical **dream-vision** poems. Later dream-visions (*The House of Fame* and *The Parliament of Fowls*) are increasingly influenced by Italian models, and the latter, a mature piece, is a minor masterpiece. Some of *The Canterbury Tales* are 'French period', such as the Life of St Cecilia and the stories of Constance and Griselda.

Chaucer's second visit to Italy in 1378 opened his eyes to a richer tradition in the work of Dante (1275–1321), whose *Commedia* he echoes many times, and Boccaccio (1313–75) whose *Teseida* and *Filostrato* became the Knight's Tale and *Troilus and Criseyde*, among his most notable poems. In these years he also translated the *Consolation of Philosophy* of Boethius (into prose) and began *The Legend of Good Women*, his last work in the French manner; like several of his works, it remained unfinished.

CHECK THE BOOK

Derek Pearsall's *The Canterbury Tales*, 1985, offers firm summaries of critical debates.

Chaucer probably began *The Canterbury Tales* in 1387, after he went into Kent. The loose narrative framework enabled him to find room for some of his old stories, and to develop his dramatic and realistic abilities. This last 'English' phase contains Chaucer's most vigorous and various work. But Chaucer was a Catholic and European as well as an English poet, and early influences are present also in the later work, although this expresses more directly his own humour and the life of his time. The dream-vision tradition, for instance, informs the structure of the Prologue. *Le Roman de la Rose* informs its characterisation and its **irony**. Chaucer is the first European writer to write in English, and in the *Tales* he gives us a comprehensive view of his world and of life in all its variety.

In Chaucer's work several traditions meet – popular, learned and courtly. He was a court poet, but had readers among the learned, the clergy and the merchant class. He had scientific and philosophical interests, yet his English is rapid, clear, unaffected and natural. He often seems as close to his audience as a popular entertainer. He would have read his work to his audience, although some would have also read him in private.

CHECK THE BOOK

Peter Brown's *The Rise of Western Christendom*, 2002, is a magnificent and authoritative introduction to the European Middle Ages.

CHAUCER'S WORLD

Chaucer's public experience of life was as a government servant and diplomat: not a courtier but a king's man. His friends were knights and London merchants. England passed through profound changes during his lifetime. In his childhood, England had great prestige, having beaten the Scots and the French in the victories of Crécy (1346) and Poitiers (1356). In 1360 France ceded much territory to England. In 1349 Edward III had founded the Order of the Garter, the first Order of Western chivalry.

But the Black Death of 1349 had killed a third of the people of England, and it returned in the 1360s. The resultant labour shortage disrupted the feudal economy. Edward III's costly war policy began to fail, and in old age the king became unpopular. Richard II came to the throne as a child in 1377 in a time of social unrest which in 1381 broke out in the Peasants' Revolt, in which, in London, John of Gaunt's palace was sacked and Archbishop Sudbury murdered in the street. There was also religious controversy: the Popes had been in captivity at Avignon since 1309, and in 1378 the Great Schism began, between rival claimants to the Papacy. The Oxford reformer, Wyclif, attacked Church abuses in the 1370s, and criticised Church dogma. Next to nothing of this gets into Chaucer's work. He shows us the greed of the new bourgeoisie, and abuses in the Church, but his religious and social values seem to be those that were usual in his day. He was certainly discreet, as befits a diplomat and a royal servant. He flourished quietly at Richard II's court, and Henry IV, John of Gaunt's son, did not reject his father's old follower when he took the throne from Richard in 1399. The history plays of Shakespeare show Richard, murdered in 1400, as the last medieval king.

Medieval society was vertically organised like a pyramid, with King and Pope at the heads of State and Church. The social hierarchy was in theory quite clear, and its ranks had legal force. People of a lower rank could be punished for wearing the dress of a higher rank. But the old feudal system, where social standing was determined by the amount of land a man held from the king, was giving way to a more open and mercantile economic pattern, especially in London, where Chaucer came from the merchant class. He was not a man of the people, but his origins were equally remote from the nobility; there are no barons among his pilgrims. His career gave him a wide experience of English life, and especially the life of London, many of whose *c.* 50,000 inhabitants he must have known. Medieval society, in spite or because of its vertical distinctions, was communal: each of Chaucer's pilgrims, however individual, is conceived of as typical of his craft or profession, and as having a rank and a role in society.

CHECK THE BOOK

In *The English Review* vol. 15, no. 1 (September 2004), a mock AS examination answer on *The General Prologue*, is 'marked' as if by an examiner, with comments.

The Christian Church was never far away from anything in Chaucer's England. A theological understanding of life had since the thirteenth century governed the interpretation put upon every physical and moral event, however material or secular its nature – whether meteorological, psychological or personal. Christian Europe was a Catholic community whose language was Latin. The Church was the same in every country, offering the same Christian social and spiritual ideal – however incompletely realised and with whatever local differences. Despite the strains which showed in the fourteenth century, with the failure of the Crusades, a weakened papacy, the Black Death, and the beginnings of less collective and more personal attitudes, there was no alternative, secular vision of life. The culture of Christendom had long offered an integration of social and religious ideals. It was a culture which gave an underlying unity, simplicity and breadth to the work of this sophisticated, adventurous and experimental writer.

RELIGIOUS LIFE

Two aspects of Catholicism may need a word of introduction:

1. Clergy are either *secular* clergy, like the Parson, who live in the world (either in major orders – bishop, priest, deacon – or 'clerks' in minor orders) or *regular* clergy. Secular priests – parish

priests – are under the supervision of the bishop of a diocese (an administrative district), and are also 'diocesan clergy'. Regulars – monks, nuns and friars – bound themselves by a Rule and lived as a community. Regulars are also known as 'religious' or 'the religious', from Latin *religio*, I bind, referring to the vows by which they have bound themselves. A regular can also be a priest – like Chaucer's Friar and perhaps his Monk. Friars, though regulars in a community, went out into the world to preach. The Summoner is a lay employee of the Church Court. The Pardoner may not have the clerical status he claims. The Knight may have been a member of a religious military order, such as the Templars or Hospitallers, or the Teutonic Knights.

2. Penance. In the New Testament, Christ says to St Peter and the apostles: 'Whose sins you shall forgive, they are forgiven.' The Church claims that priests, as successors to the apostles, have this power to offer God's forgiveness to the sinner who truly repents and performs the penance imposed. Repentance or penitence is one aim of the pilgrimage. The Pardoner has no power to absolve the guilt of sin. He deals only in certificates of remission of penance or punishment, a crucial distinction not understood by those he deceives.

CHECK THE BOOK

To read more about the seven saints mentioned in the *Prologue*, consult *The Oxford Dictionary of Saints*, ed. David Farmer, 1987

THE REFORMATION

Modern attitudes to Chaucer's Christianity and to his ecclesiastical satire, especially in England but also in other countries whose religious traditions are Protestant, are inevitably affected, not always consciously, by the series of changes which took place in the sixteenth century, known collectively as the Reformation. In the 1530s King Henry VIII ordered that he should be proclaimed head of the Church in England. While he continued to think of himself as an orthodox member of the Catholic or universal Church, his unilateral declaration of independence cut the links between the Church in England and the wider tradition of Western Christianity, and reshaped (reformed) the English Church. The Church in England was now independent of Rome, but it was subject to the monarchy. Henry's headship was despotic. He executed the most prominent of those who could not accept laws enshrining the rights of the secular ruler over the consciences of Christian subjects. Among those executed in the 1530s were Sir Thomas More, the

Lord Chancellor of England; John Fisher, the Bishop of Rochester; the monks of the London Charterhouse; and the abbots of the Benedictine monasteries of Reading, St Albans and Glastonbury, who had refused to surrender their keys to the king's agents. The Head of the Church also beheaded several men he accused of having been lovers of Ann Boleyn, and soon afterwards Thomas Cromwell, his chief agent in the the Dissolution of the Monasteries. In the short reign of Henry's son Edward VI, a boy, far-reaching programmes of Protestant doctrinal reforms were introduced by his Regents. After a brief return to Catholicism under Mary Tudor, the Protestant Church of England was finally established under Elizabeth I. Anglicanism remains the official religion of England, and was introduced into her many colonies. The Church of England retained Bishops, and a modified version of traditional Christian teaching – including her claim to be part of the Catholic apostolic Church. Yet the organisation, faith, worship, and obedience of English Christianity had been changed by compulsion. All religious orders were abolished, and each of the hundreds of religious houses in England was closed, its property confiscated and sold off. Religious images were destroyed and paintings were whitewashed. These changes ended the education and other social services provided by the religious orders. These 'reforms' were officially justified by anti-Catholic propaganda, emphasising the abuses, corruption and wealth of the clergy, and especially the landed wealth of the religious orders. The shrine of St Thomas Becket in Canterbury Cathedral, the locus of the chief pilgrimage in England, was stripped of precious metal. It was taken to London in a procession of carts retracing the route followed by generations of pilgrims, and melted down. Catholicism was outlawed, and its adherents subjected to legal penalties. In English law, the monarch, as head of the Church of England, cannot be a Catholic.

Today historians acknowledge that the break with Rome and the Dissolution of the Monasteries were politically imposed on an unwilling people. The occasion for the break was Henry's inability to secure the Church's approval for his divorce and remarriage to a (pregnant) Anne Boleyn. The child of this adulterous union, publicly repudiated as illegitimate during one of Henry's six marriages, was to become Queen Elizabeth I. A material advantage of the break was that it gave Henry an excuse for confiscating the extensive lands formerly given to monasteries.

? QUESTION
England was a Catholic country from the seventh century until the sixteenth, since then it has been an Anglican country. How does this affect the way we read Chaucer?

The reformation continued

From the Reformation until the nineteenth century, the only medieval English writer available to be read was Geoffrey Chaucer. Protestant readers could read the *Prologue*'s satire on the Prioress, Monk and Friar, and the Summoner and Pardoner, as prophetic of the Protestant Reformation, then a hundred and fifty years in the future. Some assumed Chaucer'sympathy with the reformer John Wycliffe and his followers, known as Lollards. In 1866 the Anglican divine, Frederick Denison Maurice, maintained that Chaucer was no Wycliffite. Rather, Chaucer was 'simply an Englishman. He hates Friars because they are not English and not manly.' This shows how tempting it is to read history by the light of more pressing concerns. Maurice was anxious about the the revival in Victorian England of a Roman Catholicism whose clergy, unlike the married clergy of the national Church, were celibate. Catholic religious orders of monks and friars ('not English and not manly') had started up again in England before 1800. Anglo-Catholicism had advanced so far within the Church of England that several celibate orders, chiefly of nuns, had begun to flourish. Maurice must have known that English Christianity had been Catholic for seven or eight centuries before Chaucer. He may not have reread the pages of Bede which tell how Pope Gregory had sent St Augustine and forty companions the pagan Angles in 597, or how those who had converted the English were monks from the Pope's own monastery. Insofar as it is possible to identify Chaucer's personal attitudes – which is not very far – his Christianity seems what might be expected of an educated European of his day: pious, critical of clerical abuses. F.D. Maurice, a professor of English literature at King's College, London, had presumably read the *Canterbury Tales*. These include lives of saints who were not English, and of virgin martyrs who were not manly.

CHECK THE BOOK

Diarmaid McCullough's study, *The Reformation*, subtitled *Europe's House Divided, 1490–1700*, is a good general account, published in 2003.

MIDDLE ENGLISH

Historians divide English into Old, Middle and Modern English. Old English came to an end after the Norman Conquest of Anglo-Saxon England in 1066. The rulers of England then spoke Norman French, and scholars wrote in Latin. English was spoken by most people, and gradually became a public and literary medium in the fourteenth century. Middle English was, however, an unstable mixture of dialects, infused with thousands of words from French. It was not standardised by central usage, nor by print, and changed continuously until a more stable stage was reached about 1500, when the early Modern stage of English is taken to begin. Chaucer wrote in the London dialect, from a later version of which Modern English descends.

There is no room here for an introduction to Middle English, but here are some hints:

1. Read aloud to ascertain metre and rhyme. This also helps with meaning and with tone.

2. Pronounce all consonants fully: for example the *K* and *h* in *Knight*.

3. Consult glossaries and grammatical introductions when in doubt as to sense or grammatical function.

4. Do not assume that a word means what it means today. Appearances can deceive. The *verray parfit gentil* Knight is 'true, complete and noble', not 'very perfect and soft-hearted'; '*His hors were goode, but he was not gay* means that the quality of the Knight's horses (plural) was better than that of his own attire; the *Person of a Toun* is a village parson, not an urban individual. Other examples are: *lustful* zestful; *coy* quiet; *lewed* ignorant: *girl* young of either sex; *catel* property; *smal* slender; *wife* woman; *wood* mad. Some words are loyal old friends but others are *faux amis*, treacherous friends who have changed their meanings. Words such as charity, truth, chivalry also had complex and far-reaching senses in the Middle Ages.

5. Note common words which are used in more than one sense, such as *worthy* or *gentil*, and decide on the exact sense in each instance.

6. Write your own accurate prose translation of parts of the Prologue (see **Extended commentaries, text 3** above.)

CHAUCER'S OWN ENGLISH

The best advice that can be given to a student is to make sure that he or she understands as accurately as possible exactly what

CHECK THE BOOK

Shakespeare's Chaucer: A Study in Literary Origins, Ann Thompson, 1978, is the latest study of this important relationship.

Chaucer's own English continued

Chaucer's words mean. Without an informed response to sense, there can be no sensitivity to qualities of language, nor to the poet's tone of voice. Chaucer's fresh, apt and elegant English made him a model of style. Attention to his tone of voice also gives a clue to his sense of humour. The Prologue was composed to be read aloud, and an attempt should be made to read it aloud in an approximation to the pronunciation, which can be imitated from one of the several modern recordings that have been made.

Events in Europe	Chaucer's life	Literary events
1300 Population of British Isles: *c.*5 million		
1309 Papal See moves to Avignon and comes under French Control		
		1313 Death of Jean de Meun, author of part 2 of *Roman de la Rose*, allegorical poem mocking love, women, the Church and those in authority
		1319 Death of Jean de Joinville, French chronicler
1321 Edward II forced to abdicate, imprisoned and probably murdered; Edward III accedes to throne, with wife Philippa		**1321** Death of Dante Alighieri, author of *The Divine Comedy*
		1330 Birth of John Gower, friend of Chaucer and poet
		1331 Birth of William Langland, poet
		1337 Birth of Jean Froissart, who will become Clerk of the Chamber to Queen Philippa and author of *Chronicles*, a brilliant history of 14th-century western European am chivalry
1338 Beginning of the Hundred Years War between France and England		
	1343–4 Birth of **Geoffrey Chaucer** in London	**1341** Petrarch crowned as laureate poet in the Capitol, Rome

Events in Europe	Chaucer's life	Literary events
1346 French routed at Crécy by Edward III and his son the Black Prince		
1349 Black Death reaches England and kills one third of population		
1351 First Statute of Labourers regulates wages in England		
		1353 In Italy, Giovanni Boccaccio finishes his *Decameron*, a collection of 100 tales
1356 English rout French at Poitiers		**1363** Birth of Christine de Pisan, French author of *La Cité des Dames*, listing all the heroic acts and virtues of women
	1357 Chaucer in service of Countess of Ulster, wife of Prince Lionel, 3rd son of Edward III	
1359 Edward III makes unsuccessful bid for French throne	**1359** Serves in army in France, under Prince Lionel; taken prisoner	
1360 France cedes a number of territories to England	**1360** Edward III pays ransom of £16 for Chaucer's freedom	
1361 Black Death reappears in England		
1362 English becomes official language in Parliament and Law Courts		
	1366 Marries Philippa Pan (or Payne) Roet; in Spain on diplomatic mission	
	1367 Granted life pension for his services to king; birth of his son Thomas; begins travelling abroad on King's business	

Events in Europe	Chaucer's life	Literary events
	1368 On Prince Lionel's death, his services transferred to John of Gaunt, Duke of Lancaster	
	1369 In Picardy with John of Gaunt's expeditionary force; begins *Book of the Duchess* on death of Blanche, John of Gaunt's wife	
	1370–3 Sent on diplomatic missions to Genoa and Florence	**1370 (c.)** William Langland's *Piers Plowman* (first version)
	1374 Appointed Controller of the Customs and Subsidy of Wools, Skins and Hides; receives life pension from John of Gaunt	
		1375 (c.) *Sir Gawain and the Green Knight* written
	1376 Receives payment for some secret, unspecified service	
1377 Edward III dies and is succeeded by Richard II, son of the Black Prince	**1377** Employed on secret mission to Flanders, and sent to France to negotiate for peace with Charles V	
1378 Beginning of the Great Schism; Urban VI elected Pope in Rome, Clement VII in Avignon	**1378** On diplomatic mission to Lord of Milan	
1380 John Wyclif, who attacked orthodox Church doctrines, condemned as heretic; Wyclif's followers translate Bible into vernacular	**1380** *Parliament of Fowls* written; birth of son Lewis; Cecilia Chaumpayne releases Chaucer from charge of '*de raptu meo*'	**1380s** Religious and 'Mystery' plays popular at this time
1381 Peasants' Revolt under Wat Tyler quelled by Richard II		

Events in Europe	Chaucer's life	Literary events
	1382 Appointed Controller of the Petty Customs	
	1385 Appoints deputy to perform his duties as Controller; writing *Legend of Good Women* and *Troilus and Criseyde*	
	1385–99 Living in Greenwich	
1386 Richard II deprived of power	**1386** Deprived of both official posts; elected Knight of Shire of Kent	
	1387 Wife Philippa dies; begins writing *The Canterbury Tales*	
	1388 Chaucer sells his pensions to raise money	
1389 Richard II resumes power	**1389** Appointed Clerk of King's Works at Westminster	
		1390 Gower's *Confessio Amantis*
	1391 Writes *Treatise on the Astrolabe* for 'son' Lewis; resigns as Clerk of King's Works and becomes deputy forester of royal forest at North Petherton, Somerset	
1396 John of Gaunt marries his mistress, Katherine (de Roet), Chaucer's sister-in-law		
1399 Richard II forced to abdicate; Henry IV becomes king of England		
1400 Richard II dies in prison; population of British Isles *c*.3.5 million	**1400** Death of Chaucer	**1400 (c)** Arthurian verse romances
		1450 Gutenberg produces first printed book in movable type

CHAUCER

L.D.Benson, ed., *The Riverside Chaucer*, OUP, 1987

The standard edition of his works.

Piero Boitani and Jill Mann, eds, *The Cambridge Chaucer Companion*, Cambridge University Press, 1986

Good general introduction by various hands

D.S. Brewer, *Chaucer*, 3rd revised edition, Longman, 1974

A standard general introduction.

David Burnley's *Guide to Chaucer's Language*, Basingstoke, 1983

Sets Chaucer's English agains the background of other dialects of Middle English

John Burrow, ed., *Geoffrey Chaucer: A Critical Anthology*, Penguin, 1969

An excellent selection of critical comment from early times onwards.

John Burrow, ed., *Essays on Medieval Literature*, Oxford University Press, 1984

Advanced scholarly criticism.

G.K.Chesterton, *Chaucer*, London, 1932

The last pre-academic account of Chaucer, and the best.

Steve Ellis, *Geoffrey Chaucer*, Writers and their Work, Northcote House/British Council, 1996

Brief, lively look at the works, and at the critical debate.

George Kane, *Chaucer*, Oxford University Press, 1984

A short book by a very experienced scholar.

Derek Pearsall, *The Life of Geoffrey Chaucer*, Oxford, Blackwell, 1992

Thorough, scholarly, reliable biography, with useful appendix on the Ellesmere miniatures.

D.W. Robertson, Jr., *A Preface to Chaucer Criticism*, Princeton, 1962

Learned advocacy of the case for reading medieval literature as spiritual allegory.

Beryl Rowland, ed., *Companion to Chaucer Studies*, revised edition, Oxford University Press 1979

Ann Thompson, *Shakespeare's Chaucer: A Study in Literary Origins*, Liverpool University Press, 1978

A good examination of this fascinating topic.

JOURNALS

The *Chaucer Review, Chaucer Yearbook*, and *Studies in the Age of Chaucer* are the first places in which to consult recent scholarship and criticism.

THE CANTERBURY TALES

Michael Alexander, ed., *The Canterbury Tales: Illustrated Prologue*, Scala Books, 1996

Text of Prologue with medieval illustrations in colour, including the miniatures of the pilgrims in the Ellesmere manuscript.

John J. Anderson, ed., *Chaucer: The Canterbury Tales*, Casebook Series, Macmillan, 1974

Selected critical articles.

Alcuin Blamires, *The Canterbury Tales* (the Critics Debate), London and Atlantic Highlands, NJ, 1987

A critical selection.

Harold Bloom, ed., *The General Prologue to the Canterbury Tales* (Modern Critical Interpretations), Chelsea House, 1991

Another selection of critical articles.

Muriel Bowden, *A Commentary on the General Prologue to the Canterbury Tales*, Macmillan, 1957, 2nd edition 1967

Full of detailed social history on the pilgrims' professions.

Helen Cooper, *The Structure of the Canterbury Tales*, London and Athens, GA, 1983

Persuasive scholarly criticism.

FURTHER READING

Helen Cooper, *The Canterbury Tales* (Oxford Guides to Chaucer), Oxford University Press, 1989

  Comprehensive, up-to-date, well-written and persuasive.

Ethelbert Talbot Donaldson, *Speaking of Chaucer*, Athlone Press, 1970

  Elegant and provocative scholarly criticism. ·

Kolve, V.A., *Chaucer and the Imagery of Narrative*, Stanford, California, 1984

  An account of the iconography and illustrative tradition of the first five tales

Jill Mann, *Chaucer and Medieval Estates Satire*, Cambridge University Press, 1973

  A scholarly book on the tradition inside which Chaucer was writing in the Prologue, and of the ways in which he sophisticated it.

Derek Pearsall, *The Canterbury Tales*, Allen and Unwin, 1985

  Useful scholarly commonsense discussions of the whole work.

Paul Strohm, *Social Chaucer*, Harvard University Press, 1989

  Well-informed historical scholarship and criticism.

OTHER READING

The Bible

  This should be consulted in the older translations, preferably the Douay-Rheims version, failing which the Authorised Version, which is easier to find.

Boethius, *The Consolation of Philosophy*, trans.V E Watts, Penguin Classics, Harmondsworth, 1969

John Burrow, *Medieval Writers and their Work: Middle English Literature and its Background 1100-1500*, Oxford University Press, 1982

John Burrow, *Ricardian Poetry: Chaucer, Gower, Langland and the 'Gawain' Poet*, Routledge and Keegan Paul, 1971

Peter Brown, *The Cult of the Saints*, Chicago University Press, 1982

FURTHER READING

Peter Brown *The Rise of Western Christendom*, Blackwell, 2002

J.V. Cunningham. 'Convention as Structure – The Prologue to *The Canterbury Tales*' in *Geoffrey Chaucer: A Critical Anthology*, ed., J.A. Burrow, Penguin Books, 1969, pp. 218–32.

T.S. Eliot, *The Waste Land,* Faber and Faber, 1961

David Farmer, ed., *The Oxford Dictionary of Saints*, OUP, 1987

Terry Jones, *Chaucer's Knight*, Methuen, 1994

William Langland, *Piers Plowman*, edited by A.V.C. Schmidt, Everyman, 1978.

Diarmaid McCullough, *The Reformation: Europe's House Divided*, 1490-1700, Blackwell, 2003

RECORDING

The General Prologue, read by Nevill Coghill, Norman Davis, John Burrow, 1982, Argo 1091

Much the best recording.

allegory saying one thing by means of another (Greek *allos*, other): a way of writing which allows a story to have two different meanings, as in the parables of Jesus in the New Testament; common in spiritual and moral works in the Middle Ages. George Orwell's *Animal Farm* is a modern example

alliteration a sequence of sounds beginning with the same letter (Latin *litera*), usually consonants rather than vowels; common in poetry: 'Around the rugged rocks the ragged rascal ran'

bathos (Greek, sinking) anticlimax, either deliberate or accidental. Chaucer's Merchant was a *worthy man* – but, Chaucer adds, 'to tell the truth I do not know his name'. The Cook is a good cook – but he has an unhealthy ulcer on his leg

chronographia a way of indicating time (Greek *chronos*) in writing (Greek *graph-*), usually by an elaborate circumlocution: 'When Aurora leaves the saffron bed of Tithonus' = at dawn

dialogic a name for a kind of text in which several voices can be heard; the 'dialogue' need not be explicit. (A *monologic* text would express a single viewpoint, the author's.) The word 'dialogic' is taken from the Russian critic, Mikhail Bakhtin

dream-vision a common medieval form in which the author falls asleep and dreams that he sees and describes various personifications and real persons, who talk together and to him. The dreamer seeks to learn from his experiences. Examples are the Old English *Dream of the Rood*, Dante's *Commedia*, Langland's *Piers Plowman* and Chaucer's *Parliament of Fowls*

frame-story outer story containing inset stories, as a picture-frame contains a picture

hyperbole exaggeration, a common figure of speech, as when it is said that the Wife of Bath's head-dress on Sundays weighed ten pounds

image/imagery a verbal representation or picture, either a straightforward description containing a visual element (the Yeoman has *a not heed … with a broun visage*), or a set of descriptive details making up a more complex image (as in the detailed portrait of the physically violent Miller), or the use of figurative language such as similes and metaphors

irony saying one thing while conveying something else, as when it is said that the Doctor was especially fond of gold because it was an ingredient in medicine

metaphor the description of one thing as another thing. The Miller is described as *a thikke knarre*, or knot of wood. He is not a knot of wood, but has its qualities of impenetrable toughness and awkwardness

metre (Greek *metron*, measure) the simplest quality which distinguishes verse from prose is that it has regular patterns which can be measured or counted. (This does not apply to modern 'free verse'.) 'Metre' can mean verse, or the measure used in a kind of verse. Most English verse has a number of stressed syllables in each line. The metre of Chaucer's Prologue is iambic pentameter rhyming in couplets

parody an imitation of a particular work of literature which makes fun of it by exaggerating or ridiculing its characteristic features

pentameter (Greek, five measures) a line of verse which can be divided into five feet. A foot is a term taken from classical versification (where it means a rhythmical unit with two elements notionally equal in duration) and applied to English verse. But English verse is based not on the length of syllables but on stress, beat or accent; such stresses normally alternate with unstressed syllables. An iambic pentameter is a five-beat line beginning with an off-beat

persona fictional personality who speaks in the first person. In some novels, the first-person narrator is clearly not the author. But in Chaucer's poems there is some overlap between the persona and the author, who often writes as if he is reading the poem aloud to his audience

satire the holding up of folly and vice to moral ridicule

simile (Latin *similitudo*, likeness) the likening of one thing to another; comparison using *as* or *like*. Of the Franklin it is said, *Whit was his berd as is the dayeseye*; of the Miller, *His berd as any sowe or fox was reed*

symbol (Greek, putting together) Mark, token, sign

verisimilitude (Latin 'truth-likeness'). The careful imitation of the appearance of reality in a work of fiction; an attribute of literary realism

AUTHORS OF THESE NOTES

Mary Alexander has a degree in English from the University of Melbourne and Diplomas in Education from La Trobe University and the Institute of Education, London University. She has taught English literature in schools in Australia and Britain.

Michael Alexander has recently retired from the Alexander Berry Chair of English Literature in the University of St Andrews. He has edited *The Canterbury Tales: The First Fragment* for Penguin, and *The Canterbury Tales: Illustrated Prologue* for Scala Books, and written a York Note on Chaucer's *Knight's Tale*. He has also translated *Beowulf* and other Old English poems into verse for Penguin Classics. His *History of English Literature* is published by Palgrave Macmillan.

General Editor
Martin Gray, former Head of the Department of English Studies at the University of Stirling, and of Literary Studies at the University of Luton.

Maya Angelou
I Know Why the Caged Bird Sings

Jane Austen
Pride and Prejudice

Alan Ayckbourn
Absent Friends

Elizabeth Barrett Browning
Selected Poems

Robert Bolt
A Man for All Seasons

Harold Brighouse
Hobson's Choice

Charlotte Brontë
Jane Eyre

Emily Brontë
Wuthering Heights

Shelagh Delaney
A Taste of Honey

Charles Dickens
David Copperfield
Great Expectations
Hard Times
Oliver Twist

Roddy Doyle
Paddy Clarke Ha Ha Ha

George Eliot
Silas Marner
The Mill on the Floss

Anne Frank
The Diary of a Young Girl

William Golding
Lord of the Flies

Oliver Goldsmith
She Stoops to Conquer

Willis Hall
The Long and the Short and the Tall

Thomas Hardy
Far from the Madding Crowd
The Mayor of Casterbridge
Tess of the d'Urbervilles
The Withered Arm and other Wessex Tales

L.P. Hartley
The Go-Between

Seamus Heaney
Selected Poems

Susan Hill
I'm the King of the Castle

Barry Hines
A Kestrel for a Knave

Louise Lawrence
Children of the Dust

Harper Lee
To Kill a Mockingbird

Laurie Lee
Cider with Rosie

Arthur Miller
The Crucible
A View from the Bridge

Robert O'Brien
Z for Zachariah

Frank O'Connor
My Oedipus Complex and Other Stories

George Orwell
Animal Farm

J.B. Priestley
An Inspector Calls
When We Are Married

Willy Russell
Educating Rita
Our Day Out

J.D. Salinger
The Catcher in the Rye

William Shakespeare
Henry IV Part I
Henry V
Julius Caesar
Macbeth
The Merchant of Venice
A Midsummer Night's Dream
Much Ado About Nothing
Romeo and Juliet
The Tempest
Twelfth Night

George Bernard Shaw
Pygmalion

Mary Shelley
Frankenstein

R.C. Sherriff
Journey's End

Rukshana Smith
Salt on the snow

John Steinbeck
Of Mice and Men

Robert Louis Stevenson
Dr Jekyll and Mr Hyde

Jonathan Swift
Gulliver's Travels

Robert Swindells
Daz 4 Zoe

Mildred D. Taylor
Roll of Thunder, Hear My Cry

Mark Twain
Huckleberry Finn

James Watson
Talking in Whispers

Edith Wharton
Ethan Frome

William Wordsworth
Selected Poems

A Choice of Poets

Mystery Stories of the Nineteenth Century including The Signalman

Nineteenth Century Short Stories

Poetry of the First World War

Six Women Poets

For the AQA Anthology:
Duffy and Armitage & Pre-1914 Poetry
Heaney and Clarke & Pre-1914 Poetry
Poems from Different Cultures

Margaret Atwood
Cat's Eye
The Handmaid's Tale

Jane Austen
Emma
Mansfield Park
Persuasion
Pride and Prejudice
Sense and Sensibility

Alan Bennett
Talking Heads

William Blake
Songs of Innocence and of Experience

Charlotte Brontë
Jane Eyre
Villette

Emily Brontë
Wuthering Heights

Angela Carter
Nights at the Circus

Geoffrey Chaucer
The Franklin's Prologue and Tale
The Merchant's Prologue and Tale
The Miller's Prologue and Tale
The Prologue to the Canterbury Tales
The Wife of Bath's Prologue and Tale

Samuel Coleridge
Selected Poems

Joseph Conrad
Heart of Darkness

Daniel Defoe
Moll Flanders

Charles Dickens
Bleak House
Great Expectations
Hard Times

Emily Dickinson
Selected Poems

John Donne
Selected Poems

Carol Ann Duffy
Selected Poems

George Eliot
Middlemarch
The Mill on the Floss

T.S. Eliot
Selected Poems
The Waste Land

F. Scott Fitzgerald
The Great Gatsby

E.M. Forster
A Passage to India

Brian Friel
Translations

Thomas Hardy
Jude the Obscure
The Mayor of Casterbridge
The Return of the Native
Selected Poems
Tess of the d'Urbervilles

Seamus Heaney
Selected Poems from 'Opened Ground'

Nathaniel Hawthorne
The Scarlet Letter

Homer
The Iliad
The Odyssey

Aldous Huxley
Brave New World

Kazuo Ishiguro
The Remains of the Day

Ben Jonson
The Alchemist

James Joyce
Dubliners

John Keats
Selected Poems

Philip Larkin
The Whitsun Weddings and Selected Poems

Christopher Marlowe
Doctor Faustus
Edward II

Arthur Miller
Death of a Salesman

John Milton
Paradise Lost Books I & II

Toni Morrison
Beloved

George Orwell
Nineteen Eighty-Four

Sylvia Plath
Selected Poems

Alexander Pope
Rape of the Lock & Selected Poems

William Shakespeare
Antony and Cleopatra
As You Like It
Hamlet
Henry IV Part I
King Lear
Macbeth
Measure for Measure
The Merchant of Venice
A Midsummer Night's Dream
Much Ado About Nothing
Othello
Richard II
Richard III
Romeo and Juliet
The Taming of the Shrew
The Tempest
Twelfth Night
The Winter's Tale

George Bernard Shaw
Saint Joan

Mary Shelley
Frankenstein

Jonathan Swift
Gulliver's Travels and A Modest Proposal

Alfred Tennyson
Selected Poems

Virgil
The Aeneid

Alice Walker
The Color Purple

Oscar Wilde
The Importance of Being Earnest

Tennessee Williams
A Streetcar Named Desire
The Glass Menagerie

Jeanette Winterson
Oranges Are Not the Only Fruit

John Webster
The Duchess of Malfi

Virginia Woolf
To the Lighthouse

William Wordsworth
The Prelude and Selected Poems

W.B. Yeats
Selected Poems

Metaphysical Poets